MY BEAUTIFUL
DISASTER

My brain injury, my gift, my life

DEREK
AMATO

to my children,
alex, sydney, and morgan

i am blessed with a forever growing list of people that i have and continue to share life with.

to my family, and many friends, cheers to each of you!

ONE
The Shallow End

Getting together with the guys for a barbecue and a dip in the swimming pool always seems to bring out the kid in us. I mean, c'mon, three middle-aged guys on a fall day in South Dakota, a few beers, and some great food! It's always nice to go home and visit, as there is this large group of friends that have stayed closely connected throughout the years after high school. I commonly refer to us as the "real" breakfast club.

I love seeing the changes in the city when I return to visit home. My first stop after getting settled in at Mom's is always Wayne's house. We grew up together since the sixth grade on the east side of town. We competed against each other at an early age, like every day there was sunshine, or actually, light.

Wayne's mother was pretty much in the same boat as my mom— divorced, and raising two children on her own. It was my other family. As I pulled in, Wayne was waiting to greet me; a usual hug, and then of course, I spotted the basketball. "Let's go over to the park. You up to a game? Not a one-on-one," I assured him.

My knees are a bit banged up from many years of competitive sports. Wayne never turns down a quick game. "I hope you can keep up, old man," he says to me. Laughing on our way across the street, Wayne's house is just a matter of feet from the park, and the rims even have nets.

I have always loved the sound of a basketball going through a chain net; it's a louder swoosh sound I guess. Going back and forth with banter, a bit of trash talk is always included on my end, and the results are usually even, as we both seem to try and let the other win every now and then.

After an hour and both panting with our almost fortyish kind of out-of-shape physiques, we ended up laughing during the walk back to the

1

house. My initial plan was to simply spend some time back home around the people I have truly loved. I knew it was my best support system as I attempted to outline a future career and life plan. A couple weeks can turn into a couple months real quick.

with rick and wayne for days of the new concert at nuttys bar

I knew it was time to leave, as I had spent a few months at Mom's attempting to get my life figured out. My children needed me badly, as the pressures of my ex-wife raising two daughters without me was absolutely challenging for everyone. As my fortieth birthday was approaching, I encouraged myself to get going back to Colorado, as spending my birthday with my children sounded perfect.

Leaving my job as a national corporate trainer in telecom shortly before my visit to my mother's wasn't a concern; matter a fact, quite refreshing to know I was going back to Denver to build my career consulting, in hopes of having the best of both worlds, working for myself and allowing more time for my children. I felt great, my mind seemed to be at ease from the breakup with Renee, and I was simply ready to get back to reality and the rebuilding process of my life.

"Let's go," Rick said over the phone. I will pick you up in an hour. Rick arrived; his cheery self walked in and hugged my mother, and continued to tell me we were going over to Bill's to cook and swim. Anything athletic with Rick always excited me, as he never fails to pull something crazy out of the hat, back flips on skis, back flips off cliffs, you name it, which, of course would put me into adrenalin mode.

Bill's apartment was actually quite cozy for a bachelor pad. Bill is tidy when it comes to his home. He and I always seem to find much to laugh at, regardless of the topic. I always end up laughing at Bill's laugh; he just has this infectious laugh that makes everything seem funny. There are baked beans in the oven. We have about an hour.

"Did you bring swimming trunks, Derek?" Bill asked me.

"No, I totally forgot to grab them."

"Here, put these on," he said.

As I slipped into Bill's extra pair of swimming trunks, Rick was busy in the kitchen messing with the food. The entire Sturm family can cook as well.

"I'm bringing a few beers down to the pool," Rick said.

Bill threw a towel at me, and we followed Rick out the door, as the indoor pool was a short fifty-yard walk down the hallway of Bill's apartment complex.

We snapped each other with towels as we made our way down the hallway, like typical kids preparing for pool games.

"Ouch, son of a bitch!" Rick screams out.

I had twisted my towel to provide the perfect whiplike crack that caught Rick on the back of his leg. Bill opened the doors to the pool area.

"It's all ours, there isn't anyone using the pool."

Rick immediately ran towards the pool like a little kid, then jumped into a forward flip over the water, rather the typical dive. Rick always makes anything athletic into a try that moment! Of course, we follow with valid attempts of mocking Rick's challenges.

"How about this one?" Rick says. Rick stood on the side of the pool ledge, facing backwards, stoops down, and springs up like a rocket to conquer the almighty back flip.

"Not a chance," Bill says, laughing as he makes his way over to the Jacuzzi.

"C'mon, Derek, try it!"

It doesn't take much coaxing to stimulate my challenge button, although the warm Jacuzzi looked much more inviting at the moment, so I joined Bill with a beer and relaxed for a while as we poked fun of Rick's continued boylike challenges.

Rick and I rarely saw each other anymore, as things get busy in life. Rick and I share one of those special friendships, a brother type relationship. A year or two can pass, and just as if it were yesterday, each time we see each other, there's always a consistent friendship.

One would think that years in between, struggle, hurt, loss, sickness, children, failed marriages, and so on would make you a different person, and maybe it does, but the beauty of being a part of this real breakfast club is that you are under no obligation to show up being anything other than the goofy kids we were growing up together.

I was comfortable being the jockish type of risk taker. I always seemed to take any athletic challenge and multiply it a hundred times. It's just the way I operated growing up, and still to this day. It had warmed up to be a fairly nice day, somewhere in the fifties, and I recall the TV commercial earlier in the day reminding me of the World Series game between the Cardinals and the Tigers, which I was planning on catching that evening after dinner and a swim.

Bill and I walked back up the hallway to check on the baked beans back at the apartment, and of course, Bill reprimanded me as I was sticking a fork in the pot to get a quick taste. Bill can cook a crazy good batch of baked beans.

"Get out of that. You can never wait when it comes to food, Amato."

"Let's go," Bill said, "the beans are not ready yet."

We headed back down the hallway towards the pool. Little did I know that this two-minute walk down the hallway would become the very start of the moment in my life that would simply be forgotten, or as I like to say, "That frozen space of time in between that I just can't find yet." In just two more hours, I would be dragged back down that same hallway, which would seem to take several hours!

A young man, maybe thirteen, walked in to the pool area. He was carrying a miniature football; of course, I spotted that football immediately. Rick shouted out to me once again, "I know you can't do this, Amato," as he was halfway in the air with his body in reverse just slightly above the water.

"A back flip?" I said. "That's no big deal. Do it again so I can watch, Rick." He did. I stood at the edge of the pool, with my legs prepared to launch me. I was nervous, as I had never attempted this one before. I'm going to have to really push myself outward, Rick, as I am scared that my head might hit the edge of the pool.

"Don't be a sissy," Rick said. I leaned down until my rear end almost touched the concrete. "Go!" Rick screamed. I hesitated for a moment, then bam, I hit the water. "You did it." I was kind of surprised. You get this dizzy kind of rush in mid-flip, so of course, this meant more back flips. Twenty of them later, I was tired and headed to the Jacuzzi for a breather.

The teenager would end up joining us in the Jacuzzi, clearly not knowing the sports gods he was dealing with.

"Throw me that football" I said to the teen. I knew if I waited until Bill wasn't paying attention that I could throw a spiral across the way and tag him right in the snout. The football whizzed by Bill's head.

"Hey, you asshole!" Bill screamed at me. He threw it back at me, I caught it.

Rick began to run poolside with his arms in the air. "Throw it, Derek!" he shouted as he dove over the water. Rick came plunging out of the water like a torpedo with a football in his hands.

"Good catch, Bro!"

We continued telling stories in the Jacuzzi. Dinner was almost ready, so I was ready to head back to Bill's apartment for those fantastic-smelling baked beans.

"Catch!" I warned Bill for a second attempt at throwing a bomb toward his head, barely missing. Now it became a who wasn't paying attention game, and then suddenly, the ball came whizzing by my head out of nowhere. "Someone's going to get hurt!" I shouted at Rick. We tossed the thing about between sips of beer and pretended we were still in our athletic prime performing all manner of aquatic sins, from cannonballs to belly flops.

The football rolled my way. It begged to be thrown. I wanted to catch the football one more time, this time while diving into the pool. "I can catch it while in midair," I said to Bill, "throw it." As Bill reared back to throw his best Brett Favre pass, I recall running alongside the pool. I was more in tune to making sure my diving form was perfect, rather preparing to land in the deeper section of the pool.

the football that insisted i dive

I didn't think twice, as it's very natural for me to react quickly when it comes to doing anything athletic. For that one moment while in the air, I knew I had misjudged the angle of which I would penetrate the water. I told myself quickly, *Roll onto your shoulder, it's the shallow end of the pool.* There wasn't enough time for my body to react to my thoughts, and then that sound of damage—the reality of knowing something terrible had just happened.

I exploded out of the water holding my ears. I told Rick my ears were bleeding, as I was looking into my hands as if there was blood pouring through my fingers. There was no blood. What, no blood? I told Rick and Bill that I was hurt. Bill and Rick both began saying something to me, although I couldn't hear anything, just their lips moving.

I went under the water for another short moment as I lost consciousness. Again, I came up out of the water like a propelled rocket. This time, Rick knew something was terribly wrong. The movement of the water was making me feel as if my balance was uncontrollable and shaky. I made my way to the edge of the pool reaching for Rick and Bill.

I went unconscious once again as Rick and Bill grabbed my hands and pulled me out of the water. Rick was starting to panic. After a few times in and out of consciousness, I insisted I was all right. I couldn't make sense of whose eyes I was looking into. I seized someone's arm. Immediately, the last of the afternoon light disappeared.

Rick and Bill slung my arms over their shoulders as if they were dragging me out of a war zone. The apartment was only fifty yards up the hallway. I collapsed three more times during the time they were dragging me to Bill's apartment. I recall the smell of baked beans as we entered Bill's apartment; the smell made me hungry.

"We are going to the hospital," Rick said.

"Are you crazy? I'm fine."

"Then I'm taking you to your mother's house," Rick nervously insisted.

"Where does she live?" I mumbled. Rick looked into my eyes as if he were talking to emptiness.

My life had just changed right before my very best friend's eyes.

TWO
Growing Pains

I was familiar with that thundering explosion, as the vivid memories of several head traumas from my childhood would haunt me through my growing up years. Over the decades, I've been knocked unconscious or concussed at least seven times, sometimes, mercifully, blacking out immediately, but on occasion experiencing the wretched explosion and an overwhelming sense of dread that comes from the instantaneous recognition that something very, very bad has just happened.

About thirty-two years before I had made the decision to dive into the shallow end of the swimming pool at Bill's apartment complex, I was running as fast as I could, looking into the blue sky, as the kids were screaming for me to catch it. I was in midst of catching a pop fly while playing kickball at John Marshall elementary school in southern California.

Then, suddenly, the playground monkey bars came out of nowhere, and I woke looking into the eyes of the school nurse. This was this first time I heard that crack and bang, the noise when you just know you have hurt yourself. At that moment, I became one of approximately three million people in the United States to suffer some form of traumatic head injury annually, about 300,000 of whom are left with a long-term disability. Upwards of 60,000 die—a fate, in retrospect, I'm lucky not to have stamped on my resume.

Elbows to the head during sports, head butting the concrete, and bunting baseballs with my skull certainly weren't the worst things to happen to me as a child, although, knowing what I know now, subjecting a three-pound, still developing brain to multiple hard surfaces probably didn't do me any favors! Yet, sporadic head injuries—any injury—seemed an acceptable and perhaps necessary consequence of an otherwise healthy, outdoor lifestyle for a young kid in the 1970s. Sports, especially baseball, were my focus and relished escape from the heavy responsibility of being the oldest child in a fiscally-challenged, single-parent family.

**right before my very first
solo airplane ride**

At the age of three, with my brother Dino just barely one year old, my parents divorced. We lived with Mom, but Dad remained an almost regular presence in the early part of our lives, taking Dino and me along to the karate studio with him daily to train from the moment we could walk. Occasionally we'd dine with him—the mealtime governed by a kitchen timer programmed to exactly twenty-seven minutes in order to prevent us from indulging in horse play at the table.

As imposing as dad was, he never hit us; that was Mom's last resort. When we were unbearably badly behaved, she'd break out one of those floppy orange tracks from a Hot Wheels set and whack us on the rear end. Despite the tough love, we adored her, still do. She was beautiful, tender (sans Hot Wheels tracks), and ever-encouraging.

We were never starved of affection as kids, although heat, food, and money were a different matter. Mom decided to take us boys back to the Midwest, where she had her parents and siblings. Moving into the apartment on the east side in Sioux Falls would be the beginning of a fantastic and challenging growing up.

Mom did her best, sometimes working two or three jobs at a time to try and make ends meet. As a result, I spent a lot of time looking after Dino and, from the age of six or seven, basically managing the household: cleaning our modest two-bedroom apartment, washing, helping dress my brother and preparing whatever food we had in the place.

An abiding memory is frequently adding water in the absence of prohibitively expensive milk to Dino's stale cereal. Winters were toughest. We seldom had enough money to pay for utilities, so we'd spend chilly nights wrapped in every available coat and blanket. Through many of those years, I'm guessing up until around twelve to thirteen years old, we shared a bed, simply due to space and not having three beds between us all. And like all kids, we would sneak in to curl up with Mom. Sharing the couch with her for Johnny Carson would become the thing to do.

my brother dino after burning his fingers from touching the b-day cake candles

Always sure of myself as to what to do when relieved of my responsibilities, I'd immediately head outside, to run, throw, tackle, jump, climb, wrestle ... I relished physical exertion and, as far back as I can remember, competition. I played harder than any other six-year-old and had the bruises to prove it.

The headaches started when I was about nine years old. Maybe I used to blow fuses: overextend myself. Whatever the reason, I had head pain with uncommon regularity as a little boy, prompting Mom to seek barely affordable medical advice.

Of course, doctors initially waved it off as a symptom of growing and, to be honest, the headaches were almost tolerable because it would give me a chance to forego the chores and luxuriate in Mom's close, personal care.

She'd rub my temples and squeeze the back of my neck for hours to alleviate the pain and take the opportunity to remind me of how much she valued what I did at home.

"You're a special boy, Derek. You were put here to do amazing things," she'd purr.

What qualified as "amazing" in my mind, for the longest time, was the ability to throw a 95 mph fastball and sure enough, I was on track, right from the earliest years, to achieve that lofty goal.

While most first grade kids were busy throwing tantrums, I was hurling baseballs. As a seven-year-old, I could put a pitch by the best and burliest twelve-year-old 'power hitters.'

I lived for Saturday morning baseball, tournaments, and anything to do with being on the dirt playing ball. Mom, despite being a slave to multiple employers, would always manage to shake free to be in the stands with Dino to watch me. I felt a great need to excel for her; for my brother. It was us against the world, and the world didn't have a chance if I was pitching.

I recognized pretty early that sports, primarily baseball, was my ticket to popularity, both as a kid in California and when we moved to Sioux Falls. Rather than have to engage in that complicated business of making friends, I'd just play sports better than anybody else to ensure I was the center of attention.

Being a swaggering, elementary school jock planted the seed for me to later become a rebellious and belligerent teen, although I was always usually pretty compliant around the family. At home, I was the dutiful son: man-of-the-house even, seldom ignoring my obligations, ensuring the care of my younger brother. It just felt natural to love, care, and nurture others. I suppose it's all those experiences that color my currently grown up soul today.

Without hesitation, I also spent a lot of time with Mom caring for her cerebral palsy and muscular dystrophy-afflicted sister, JoAnne. My grandparents raised Deborah, who JoAnne gave birth to in the sixties. The enormity of my aunt's burdens has never been lost on me—the terror, confusion, and loneliness she must have endured at times in her life. I didn't know all the details back then, but I was unfailing as her ten-year-old defender, anxious to shield her from the torture of teasing.

Every weekend, we would visit my grandparents in the small town of Irene, South Dakota. Sunday mornings at the Lutheran Church as I'd sit next to my grandmother Olga as she assaulted the organ with a mixture of musical fervor and religious zeal, and later listen intently as Grandpa Joe, the chief of police, would relate homespun parables gleaned from witnessing the sins of the riff-raff around town.

With a population of 425 people, I never did get a chance to chase any bad guys in the police car with my grandfather—although, many times, I would sit with him at night and pretend we were going to have to arrest someone speeding through town. Grandfather Joe was a genuinely kind man. I learned much from him.

So was it on a steamily hot summer's day—game day. Celebrating a baseball victory with my teammates meant being as unruly as a ten-year-old could be long after the game. Mom had headed out, leaving me with my buddies after Mac, my friend Tommy's dad, had promised to get us home in his pickup. Sure enough, five of us boys jumped in and headed for home.

Safety standards in those days weren't the greatest, but even at the time, we sensed that sort of ride could be foolhardy. A couple of times on the way home, Mac gave us a stern lecture about staying seated when the pickup was moving.

However, as the go-to guy on the team, it fell to me to stand up as the truck was stuttering along for longer than anyone else. I achieved my goal and, a few blocks away from my house, decided to go out in a blaze of glory.

As the truck pulled up to our neighborhood, we were only a few blocks from my apartment; I jumped off, generating a burst of mischievous squeals and hoots of admiration from my friends. The truck wasn't going very fast, I'm guessing around 10 mph.

I sailed toward the grass strip, parallel to the sidewalk, but before I could set myself for a safe landing, the road came up to greet me.

Crack. Boom!

Apparently, the truck just kept on clattering along. My disappearance was explained away: I had jumped off just as we came upon the intersection a few blocks before my apartment, and was now probably getting a soda from the store, a favorite place we would go to get candy.

In fact, I may have been knocked unconscious on the side of the road at that time. I don't know. I can't remember. I later established a few people saw what happened and tended to me.

Seems I had my reply down pat and shooed them away with "I'm okay" before staggering off, in the wrong direction On reflection, a lifetime later, about the only thing I'm sure happened was the quarter of an inch protection my skull offers my brain had been called into action ... once again.

On impact, the fragile, jelly-like brain, hosting about 100 billion nerve cells, covered in a fibrous substance and swilling about in protective fluid, likely smacked into the front part of my skull as my hard head and the much harder road went at it.

Tissue and blood vessels would have been buffeted, stretched and smashed around the point of impact. As my head rebounded off the ground, it's quite likely my (literally) bouncing brain slammed into the back of my skull, potentially causing a coup-countercoup injury, probably contusions.

Chances are the axon stems that send signals along the 300 billion or so brain cells and the dendrites, the receivers of the signals, would have been strained and possibly sheared in the impact, releasing toxic chemicals, potentially killing neurons and impacting communication in the brain—the bank of all memories, interpreter of sensory information and director of movement—in the short, medium, and long term.

The good news is I got home, albeit about two hours after the accident, having wandered around in a daze for several blocks before finally stumbling in. I tried to fudge my way through the explanation of why I was late, cut, bruised, and disoriented, and I remember working to convince Mom I didn't need to be taken to hospital.

Just a rub of the temples and a neck massage would be enough, I insisted: "You're a special boy, Derek...."

But no, not this time. She loaded me in the car and sped to the emergency room. Apparently, I kept telling her to slow down. Upon arriving at the hospital, I was demanding to talk to my dad in California and badgered the nurses for chocolate and banana popsicles.

Despite my insistence to anyone who would listen that I was just fine, I was formally diagnosed with a serious concussion for the first time in my life.

It took a few weeks of rest, frequent temple rubbing, and tantrums about missing baseball drills before things returned to 'normal.' I resumed squeezing school in between my sports commitments, sang in the choir at church on Sundays, visited JoAnne and occasionally got to sit in Grandfather's patrol car and stalk the Irene criminal element. (It didn't quite measure up to the excitement you come to expect from TV cop shows, as watching the show *Barretta* was my favorite thing to do, it reminded me of my father.)

However, something was amiss. I still can't put my finger on it, but the fallout from the pickup truck tumble impacted me for longer than it should have. The obvious conclusion is it shook something loose 'up there' and, indeed, the headaches became more frequent and intense. The smell and taste of gasoline and car exhaust became a frequent episode, which I would later in life be told that this experience would be considered "synesthesia." But more than the physical ramifications, it was as if I were suddenly adrift—a lot of the fun went out of life, and I'm not sure that should happen to any ten-year-old.

My baseball training went up a notch, perhaps both a curse and a blessing. Having shown considerable raw talent since I was five, I was now being formally groomed to succeed on the mound. My coach, Don, would pick me up five days a week after school and I would throw 75 pitches every day.

It was grueling, although I appreciated the opportunity to focus on something other than looking after Dino and dealing with headaches. I'd always breezed through school, but suddenly that was becoming a burden, too.

Our tight little family was the comfort zone, yet even that would be tested. Grandma Olga was sick one night, sending Mom, Dino, and me over to look after her and keep her company.

with my grandmother Olga

During the next few weeks, my concern for my grandmother's health would lead me to a beginning struggle with depression. It wasn't the fact that she was ill, it was simply dreadful watching my mother hurt as her mother began to slip away.

I wasn't ready for the loss of my grandmother, and I couldn't stand the fact that Sunday mornings sitting next to her at the organ would be stripped away from me so early in my life.

My mother would load us boys up in the car some two weeks later. "We are going to stay with grandma and grandpa for awhile," telling us how important it was for us to be there to care for her mother.

It was somewhat exciting to know that we would be living in such a small town, as the first thing that came to my mind was, *I can't wait to get on the baseball field!* as I knew the small town only had so many kids to compete with, and I would surely stand out.

The growing pains in my knees and right shoulder continued to escalate, not to mention the depression setting in as grandma's fragile presence began to wither. I just couldn't deal with watching my mother hurt so bad. "I need something for the pain, Mom," as I begged for relief from my overexerted young body, which was already banged up far more than most kids my age.

Mom had no choice but to consult doctors. After several visits to a variety of "experts," I was prescribed with narcotic painkillers.

I fully suspect that the wholesale prescription of drugs such as Percocet and Hydrocodone for a ten-year-old would be frowned upon these days (and if not, why not?) Even back in the '70s, it was probably unusual, but the power of medical authorities and their elixirs was rarely questioned in suburban America.

I was desperate for *help*, so anything offering a change would have been acceptable. I suspect Mom felt the same way and with doctors providing limited guidance, there was no doubt we turned a blind eye to the possible ramifications.

A few times, the pain was so bad she whisked me to the emergency room where doctors administered morphine. I have very little memory of those occasions.

Narcotic pain relievers attached themselves to pain receptors and modify (numb) the message that something is wrong with the body while releasing endorphins to generate a feeling of euphoria.

The flow of endorphins from narcotics far exceeds the body's natural level of production, ensuring the brain quickly becomes dependent on the relative tidal wave of chemically induced reactions to mask the pain and induce that woozy feeling of well-being.

The drugs do this questionable intervention in a part of the brain that is still growing in kids and, over time, they potentially impact the ability to make choices and weigh judgments. For decades afterwards, I was the classic exemplar of this.

Perhaps shockingly, a quick visit to a doctor, every so often, was enough to get a steady, solid supply of the pernicious pills, but even if I ran out, I quickly became aware they were available from my preteen peers in our corner of Sioux Falls. Mom had no idea I was topping myself up and I just didn't care to think about any consequences.

Obviously, we were painfully ignorant of the potential fallout from using strong medication. The compelling point was that it seemed to work, making it possible for me to function, that is, play and practice baseball, at a high level.

There is no doubt I numbed some physical pain that I may have been better off experiencing as my body was growing, but I didn't want to let the coaches down and pitching was my calling card.

By the time I was twelve, I had broken most every local pitching record: was irrefutably on track to being a star player and unquestionably becoming hooked on narcotic painkillers.

Thirty five years later, I'm not so sure if I was taking the pain medication for my hurting body. Maybe it was simply a young man's way out of dealing with the early pressures of life struggle, atop my aching and already beat up athletic physique.

Either way, my young life became blurry during my relationship with those little white pills.

THREE
Point Me in a Direction

I rolled in and out of consciousness a few times in Bill's apartment. The smell of the casserole cooking didn't help my nausea.

I had apparently managed to walk part of the 40-yard trek to the apartment using my friends as crutches. I collapsed again as we entered, which can be the only possible explanation for me ending up with my head buried in bachelor Bill's comfortable couch.

There was talk of ambulances, hospitals ... that food smell was everywhere.

We all apologized to each other for what had happened, lamenting not having sat around inert as men of our age should, and the guys constantly reminded me how lucky I was my head hadn't split open like a dropped melon.

The smell of those damn baked beans would stay with me to this very day: I just wanted to get out of there, but "no hospital, just take me to Mom's."

It was my lifelong default reaction to getting knocked unconscious: just get me home, where I could get a little TLC, a rub on the temples and a squeeze to the back of the neck and everything would be all right.

Of course, when walking into my mother's house, she immediately had that puzzled look on her face. "What happened, you guys?" Rick explained that I had hit my head while diving into the swimming pool.

That frantic voice appeared again. I was so familiar with this tone of concern, as my mom telling Rick to help get me to the car. Once again, I found myself telling Mom it was no big deal. "We're almost there," she said, speeding all the way until pulling up to the emergency doors.

"We are going to need a wheelchair," my mother told the security man. I'm not getting in that thing. I can walk on my own, as the wheelchair simply looked debilitating.

She insisted, I sat, and the items and people we passed seemed as moving colors in frozen time.

There is a consistent pattern amongst those of us that suffer a head trauma. I was not only convinced I was fine, but I was, from my understanding, very challenging to deal with. I suppose this was the doctor's way of politely saying, "This guy is being difficult"—all of which doctors completely understand, of course.

Early morning came; I was becoming more irritable as time went by. I was tired and exhausted. I couldn't make any sense of why my mind was racing and I couldn't place my thoughts around understanding what had happened while over at Bill's house.

"You need to lay still, Derek," again, Mom reassuring she was next to me. My hands were continually searching for a place to rest, as my fingers had this feeling of restlessness. "Son, stop moving your fingers so much and relax."

I closed my eyes. "Why are we here?" I once again insisted, eager to leave the hospital.

"I will wake you when it's time to go." I dozed off to sleep.

I woke up in the morning feeling relatively good. Four days later, I'd lost ninety or so hours, although not all of it to sleep. Apparently, I'd made a decent fist of feigning cognizance, functioning at some level with my eyes open for long stretches over several days.

I recall being woken by Mom about every two hours or so. There was a moment when I caught her staring at me as she thought I was sleeping. I opened my eyes to the stare only a mother in search of her son could describe. It was a sad and lost look, as if she were looking into me hoping for a normal response.

There was a connection when Mom was looking down at me waiting for a response. Even while there was no exchange of words during that brief moment, again, it was that familiar experience of "frozen time," everything just still, no sound, just my voiceless mind examining that three-second moment as if it were an hour exploration. It was as if I were screaming through my eyes saying "I'm okay."

I look back at that frozen moment in time often, and, for some reason, there is this strong connection my mind has with trauma. It's an energy my mind seems to connect with when I am presented with a person who is damaged from a trauma situation. It's a clear understanding, an immediate bond in some cases, and even at times so strong it literally makes me noxious and physically drained. I feel their presence in a different way since my accident.

Five years after my diving accident, my phone would ring as I stood on the deck looking out at our endless strip of trails, as the house sits just west of Ft. Collins in the middle of the foothills. I didn't take the call as I was getting ready to eat dinner, and I didn't recognize the number. Josh had potatoes on the oven and steaks on the grill, a very common evening of cooking together. My phone rang again just minutes after the first attempt. "Good evening," I answered, still standing on the deck.

"Is this Mr. Amato?" It was a serious voice I didn't recognize.

"It is," I replied with some hesitation in my voice.

"We need you to come to the emergency center right away."

Immediately, my mind went once again into that "frozen time" moment. "Pardon me?" I asked.

"Your son has been transported to Heart of the Rockies Medical."

"My son?"

"He was involved in a high-speed rollover and was ejected from the vehicle."

"Is he alive?"

I collapsed to my knees, hanging onto the deck railing. Josh came out.

"Are you okay, Derek?"

Looking up to Josh, I couldn't speak. After an immediate understanding that something was wrong, he put his hands on my shoulder to make sure I didn't fall over. I was still kneeling with the phone to my ear.

"Is he alive?" I asked the officer calling me.

"I can't tell you anymore than that, Mr. Amato. I suggest you leave immediately."

I must have asked ten times if my son was alive before hanging up after getting directions. I knew the area, as Alex had just been transferred out to the mountain regions for his job. "Josh, call my brother. There's no way I could operate a motor vehicle at this moment."

I was scrambling now some two minutes after the call. I called my mother, who began crying before I could even finish telling her of the situation. I was in a frantic mode to get a hold of the immediate people who needed to know what was going on—Mom, my ex wife, etc.... I couldn't get myself to call my daughters, as I knew this news would shatter them.

"Let's go, Derek!" Josh screamed from the kitchen. "Throw some stuff in an overnight bag, your brother is meeting us at the freeway." It was a fifteen-minute drive down the mountain, then another twenty-five minutes through town to the freeway. I don't recall the drive to meet my brother; actually, I recall very little of the four-hour drive to get to the hospital.

Josh gave me a hug as I got into my brother's vehicle; everyone seemed in reaction mode, I was spinning. My mind was overwhelmed with the pace of music being composed, and with the trauma forcing my mind to attempt to focus, I had become overstimulated to the point of having literally no clarity and understanding of the next four-hour drive.

"Watch for deer," my brother instructed. Night driving though the Rocky Mountains is absolutely dangerous. There is wild life everywhere, and the deer jump in and out of the road faster than you can possibly react.

"How much further?" I asked my brother.

"We just left forty minutes ago, Derek."

"I thought we were close."

"About four more hours. Don't worry, it's going to be all right."

Things were flying right by me, as my mind was now overstimulated to the point of deliriousness. I kept telling my brother to drive faster, I was getting frustrated at how long the drive was becoming. I didn't know what to do with my racing thoughts, my fingers seemingly working at a lightening pace on my legs as if they were piano keys.

"We're almost there, Derek. Relax, Brother, you have to focus." Pulling into the emergency center seemed surreal, as the evening glow over the little town seemed orange with brilliant blue skies, almost too picturesque for the moment.

My door opened as we parked. "Hold on, Derek, let me park." Walking towards the hospital doors was more of a feeling of walking down death row towards the gas chamber. Pure fright overwhelmed me as I wobbled towards the entrance. My brother scrambled to catch up to me. He grabbed my arm to make sure I didn't fall down.

There seems to be a special and immediate connection among the physicians and family members when trauma is present. Walking in through the doors, I made eye contact with the attending physician. He had given me that look, you know, maybe it's a father-to-father moment, I'm not sure. He gave me that "It's okay" look. He swung open the curtain, surrounding my son as he assisted me into the room. I immediately broke down, asking everyone to leave the room. I can be a fairly intense person when it comes to moments like these. The physicians and staff understand this process well with family members, and to my recollection, they handled me in a most comforting way.

"Please, don't physically touch your son, Mr. Amato."

"What do you mean?"

"His body is badly swollen."

How does a father walk into a hospital room with his child hooked up to tubes, a neck brace, and a swollen body that is hardly recognizable, and not put his hands upon his child? It seems only natural for parents to reach for the physical feeling of giving the child validation of their presence. I sat staring at Alex for several minutes, begging God as tears rolled down my cheeks. I wanted to put my hands upon him so badly that I was becoming angry—angry enough to produce that rare moment when I taste exhaust.

I whispered in my son's ear to let him know I was there. There was no reaction, and my whispers quickly became demands. "Don't you leave me, Alex," I insisted. I was getting sick, and my mind wouldn't allow me to find any sense of control, a true moment of helplessness.

my son alex just hours after his car accident in the mountains

I was so eager to let my son know I was there, that I recall racing thoughts of how do I connect with my child, I can't even put my hands upon him. I must have sat there crying for a solid ten minutes. I got it, it struck me. I know he will feel me breathing. I leaned over as close as I could get my face to his, laying my head on the same pillow as his battered head and face. My mouth almost touched his ear. I couldn't speak by this time, as that quiet cry engulfed my whole being. I simply began to breathe against my son's face. I knew he could feel my presence. The doctors came in shortly after, asking me to step out. I joined my brother outside the room. Dino was staggered, as this was the most intense trauma he had experienced with one of my children. He and Alex have a very special bond, very much a fatherly type of thing, Alex adores my brother; they have an understanding, if you will.

"I can't do this," I told my brother.

"You're all right, Derek, he will get through this. He's a tough kid."

Alex had lost control of his SUV going through the mountain pass on his way home from work. I was instructed by the officers that his vehicle went off the road, rolled several times, and he was ejected from the vehicle at high speed, leaving him many yards from the vehicle. Alex had somehow crawled toward the edge of the road out of the ditch. He recalled choking on his blood as his mind worried about not being able to see his son again; he knew he was damaged terribly bad.

Alex went unconscious, although he could hear a gentleman speaking to him. He was going in and out now. How ironic that way out in the middle of nowhere, forty minutes from civilization, the person who would pull over to assist my son would be a physician. He covered Alex, assuring him that help was on the way. After loading him into the ambulance, Alex recalled voices, although, the attending EMTs were certain he was unconscious. "We have to hurry, we are losing this kid!" Alex heard this conversation, but he was not coherent enough to say anything. Alex somehow told them to call me as he drifted in and out, the ambulance doing their best to get him quickly to the hospital.

My mind was now going over and over, attempting to process all of this, my head still on his pillow, doing my best to breathe against my son's face, begging him to feel my presence. He opened his eyes, blood and swelling giving him just enough space to peek through. Finally, a connection—that same look my mother gave me just five years back. I understood it now. It's a peaceful moment. It's validation.

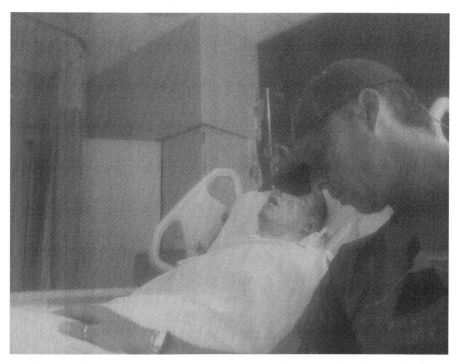

praying

I would spend the next four months of my life assisting my child back to health, an experience that now would give us both much to be grateful for, a bond far beyond my expectations, and I remind myself how lucky I am to still have my son. Thank you for listening, God!

Mom said I puttered about between sleeps for the next few days, saying little and not making a whole lot of sense when I did. She told me I had to return to the hospital for a checkup in a few days.

As day four passed, I had spent most of the time sleeping. It was now day five. I was eager to get up, almost as if late for work.

"Why don't you relax, Derek, and I will make you breakfast." Coffee chat with my mother has gone on for many years. It's our moment to catch up, start the day on the phone together, as living a distance away has never interrupted our morning process.

I glanced at myself in the mirror.

"Must have had a bad accident," I told Mom as if she hadn't noticed the bulbous swelling all over my face and the green-blue bruises under my eyes.

My neck hurt and I had a problem hearing properly. Everything was muffled on the left side, as if someone had stuffed gobs of cotton into my ears.

The memory of the pool incident seeped back, as did the sense of urgency about getting home to Denver.

"Just relax and recover," Mom said. "Everything will still be here in a few days."

But I couldn't. It wasn't only Denver making me anxious; everything seemed overwhelming, lurching out of control.

I tried to lock in on what was going on. The loss of hearing inexplicably had something to do with it, I was sure.

Gradually, like eyes adjusting to the dark, I started to focus on what was making me uneasy. My mind was racing, bunches of thoughts competing for limited spots—a game of musical chairs in the mind. I realized if I let it wash over me, it wasn't so breath-depriving and unpleasant; in fact, it felt briefly invigorating.

I was rebooting.

FOUR
Cover-Up

The pain medication became a slowly growing problem during my athletic teen days. I remained on an upward trajectory in sports, but I was still dealing with injuries, headaches, and enduring the emotional fallout from not having a father figure present.

I wasn't necessarily a rebellious kid—I had too much responsibility at home for that—but I was seeking an outlet, a release. The scent of marijuana drifted into my life and I inhaled. I was twelve years old.

The great stabilizers in my life were the strong women surrounding me growing up: My mother and grandmother counseled me to continue to believe anything was possible and urged me to seek the guidance of God. Mom was never a bible thumper; rather, she was a conservative Lutheran Midwestern girl who would do her best to make sure we were raised with faith.

Whatever was happening Sunday at the Lutheran church was a constant. I would snuggle up to my grandma on the seat at the church organ, a beast of an instrument only she could tame, as this would become my safe haven.

growing up at Eastside Lutheran

It was captivating, even for a pot-smoking twelve-year-old, as Grandma would belt out a hymn and complement her keyboard skills with a wobbly but melodic vibrato. Mom and Grandma encouraged me to learn to play the organ, but I would have none of it: singing hymns was one thing, but getting that instrument to groan wasn't my style. My musical tastes were far more contemporary.

I became friends with Curt Weidenbach in the summer of sixth grade. Wayne, Curt, and I all went to different elementary schools, all of which blocks from one another. My mother was managing a bar just a couple miles up the hill from the house we were renting on Sixth Street. Curt and I became very close during junior high school.

I spent the night one evening at Curt's during a school night. "We should sneak into the bar tonight after they close," I suggested.

"Are you crazy?" Curt insisted, although with that curious teenager tone.

"We can sell a few of those bottles of booze for ten bucks apiece. It must have been around 3:00 am.

"Let's go then."

Curt and I quietly made our way out of the house. At that time, kids could get their drivers' license permit at fourteen years of age.

We parked in the back, nervously watching for cops. It was dark when we entered, and the stagnant smell of cigarettes and booze is still etched in my mind to this day. We scurried through the bar to the back storage room.

"How many bottles should we take?" Curt asked.

"I don't know; maybe five."

We ended up taking ten bottles of liquor. We told a few kids at school the next day that we could get a bottle of booze for ten dollars. The buzz was out quickly, and we quickly made 100 bucks. I hid thirty dollars in my mom's purse, and Curt and I kept the rest. This happened a few times during junior high school.

Curt and I weren't meant to be robbers, although bootleggers? Sitting in class that day, someone passed a note to me. "The bottle broke in his gym bag in class. There is slow gin everywhere in the boys' locker room." We never got ratted out, and I can't even remember who got caught, but it was enough to scare us straight, and our bootlegging days came to an abrupt halt. I would later in life tell my mother of my crimes over coffee. She was disappointed to say the least.

Curt bought a guitar. He belonged with a guitar in his hands. Ripped jeans, a Metallica t-shirt, and he just had that look of a young rock star in the making. Before you knew it, Curt was learning to play all the rock songs I loved—"Smoke on the Water," "You Really Got Me," "Paranoid...." I loved Ozzy Osbourne and idolized his guitar player, Randy Rhodes.

The only thing more musically demonstrative than an electric guitar was a drum kit, and one, somewhere, had my name written all over it. Mom had bought me a snare drum in the sixth grade in hopes to occupy some of my time with school band. It didn't really work out— seemed to take way more effort to learn how to read music than it would take to stand on a stage someday and act like a rock star.

I shared our emerging passion to be rock stars with only a few people, among them a local 7-11 store manager, Norm Baily, who gradually became my confidante.

Norm was a gentle, thoughtful man who, unlike every other male in town, wasn't preoccupied with using me to chase after my attractive mother.

Norm would often take Wayne, Dino, and me to a ball game, the movies, or the sprint car races, but as importantly, lend his ear to me, no strings attached.

Norm had become a father figure to me well before he purchased my first and only drum kit. Curt and I persuaded Jimmy to join us in this rock star status in junior high school. Even though it would be a short lasted musical journey, it was the beginning of friendships that would still be present in my life some thirty years later.

My junior high school years were by far my most favorite memories growing up. There were several influential people who became instrumental in my daily life. Kathy Goss would scold me for constantly chatting and being interruptive in class. I enjoyed this process with her, as, at the end of every school day, I would always stop into the class room with Kim to say goodbye to Kathy.

I would end up going back to Wittier junior high many times for that "moment with Kathy" during my high school years. I always enjoyed seeing Kathy, and to date, still friends we are. Kathy always believed in me and my dreams growing up. Even with that firm look she would give me during class when I was a bit challenging, it always ended with a smile.

"Grab your baseball stuff, Derek, Don is going to be here for practice!" Mom yelled out.

"I don't want to go today, Mom … I'm tired and sore. None of the other kids are practicing today, it's Saturday morning," I whined.

"He will be here in fifteen minutes, get up and going," she reminded me.

Growing pains in my knees and shoulders were consuming my body when not actually playing or competing. It would hurt to the extent where I recall many nights of crying myself to sleep, rather than asking Mom to take me to the hospital. Mom would usually hear me whimpering in the middle of the night. She would come in and rub my aching shoulder and knees until I would finally fall asleep from exhaustion. I never considered taking large amounts of narcotics at one time. It would usually be the prescribed amount.

"Don is here, Derek."

I grabbed one pill, washed it down with a little milk, and I was out the door to once again make the best attempt to be the best baseball player on the planet.

Don was usually quite aggressive verbally. He pushed me in a different way than all the other players on the team. I knew he was grooming me into a pitching monster, but the consistent bitching and telling me I had to throw harder, snap my wrist more, and follow through, and … basically overworked my young growing body, but my curve ball would scare the hell out of any batter at that age.

I always wanted Randy Kouri as my baseball coach growing up. Randy was a tremendous figure to all of us kids who played ball together. He was a balanced coach, and certainly intense he could be, but there was a certain understanding Randy had with the kids he coached. I finally got Randy as a coach after I was selected for the all-star team. This was one of the highlights of my baseball playing years. It was a team of, in my humble opinion, the best of the best. I felt lucky to be on this team. We went on to win the state and regional championships, ending in Salina, Kansas. I threw a one hitter that day, of course in pain.

Earlier in the day, I had mentioned my elbow was killing me and I didn't think I could throw that day. Don immediately grabbed me by the arm and said, "Let's go for some therapy." I thought he was going to rub my elbow out, the usual process. We approached the bathrooms on the baseball complex. I wasn't sure what the hell was going on—a bathroom? Don reached over and flushed the toilet, and then flushed it again. "Put your elbow down in the toilet," he ordered.

"What? Right in the toilet?" I asked.

"Hurry up, we have to have you ready to go."

The toilet therapy process would become a signature among my peers and plenty of ammo for teen banter. "It's really damn cold!" I told Don.

"It's not only cold, the toilet flushing makes a vortex that pulls on your tendons and muscles," he assured me.

Sure enough, about twenty flushes later, my elbow was numb as it could be. I stepped on the mound and threw one of the best games of my young career; although the pain I endured toward the end of the game would plague any chances of playing college baseball, it was the most challenging moment physically that I had ever endured.

I reached down to remove my cleats. My right hand was shaking to the point of not being able to physically grasp my shoelace. My shoulder was pounding with pain, as I could feel my heart beat, making my shoulder pulsate in sync. I couldn't extend my right arm in my second attempt at taking off my dirty cleats, and of course, ended up simply kicking them off with my feet.

The other kids were celebrating our win. They were running around the field, taking pictures, the coaches shaking all the parents' hands, as I was sitting in the dugout, making very slow progress just getting into a pair of tennis shoes. I wanted to join the other kids, as the laughter and banter was pulling at me to join in.

Randy Kouri walked over to the dugout. "You all right, Derek?"

"I'm trying to get my shoes on, my shoulder isn't cooperating." Randy simply knew I was hurting. I could tell he was frustrated at how hard Don would push my every limit on the mound.

"He can't have you throwing so many curve balls, Derek. Here, let me help you." Randy grabbed my shoes and started putting them on for me.

Randy, Kim, and Bryan Kouri

"You know, Derek, you can practice once a week and be a good athlete, and you can practice every day and be a great athlete. I think you're one of the great ones."

I thanked Randy for helping me with my shoes. I would see Randy periodically through the years, mostly a run in at the YMCA. The Kouri family inspired me during my growing up years. Randy was someone I always adored. I received an e-mail from Randy's children not long ago that he had passed away. I sat and cried. I would later go on to tell my son Alex during our father/son coaching years the very same thing: "I think you're one of the great ones, Alex." Alex would follow my exact baseball footsteps growing up, only as a lefty—and yes, even a few elbow flushes in the toilet!

After Randy went back to join the other coaches, I quietly made my way to the bathroom for a few more numbing flushes for the elbow—and a pill, of course....

More hurt was on the way.

FIVE
The Gift

As the day progressed, the relax-and-enjoy-it phases would last a few minutes, only to be overwhelmed again by the sense of drowning in a torrent of information.

I couldn't pull the reins on what was galloping through my mind. It was an insanely exaggerated version of what happens when you're tired and you can't focus properly on one thing. Concepts would pop into my head, only to be immediately elbowed out of the way by another partial thought.

Amid the mania, I concluded I had no option but to try and get back to Denver; if not tomorrow, the day after. I'd mentioned wanting to leave to Rick who, of course, suggested I say a quick final farewell.

Rick stopped over to pick me up. "Let's go, I want to show you the boat I just finished building." The prairie house is large, and Rick only uses the two rooms: one to sleep, and one to play his guitars in.

As usual, the prairie house was a visual cacophony: musical instruments and amplifiers scattered all over, and the remains of the sustenance of choice for middle-aged musicians everywhere: junk food and liquor, leaving a kind of bread-trail around the space—evidence of where Rick has been sitting at various stages over the last four hours.

"Rick, what the hell is that? Is it a spaceship on the wall?"

There was this abstract structure of oddly cut foam pieces, and of course, due to Rick's creative and artistic mind, the structures were not only art on the wall, but sound dampening items to absorb guitar amplification when the knob is set to 11. There was also a photo of Rick's father, Gene, on the wall with a tack holding it up.

Gene was always a strong male figure to me growing up. Always pleasant, but firm. On Sundays, we would visit Gene. It would be the usual—me, Rick, Randy, Mike, and sometimes Patrick. The Sturm family is an eating and cooking family. A fond memory I have of the Sturm kitchen when over at the house was, on a certain day of the week, Rick's parents saying, "It's *Musgo* tonight!" I always found it funny to hear, and Gene would concur, "Everything in the fridge musgo."

Back to Sunday, as a scotch and a few beers would always be on hand for a brunch. I have never been a big drinker, but occasionally, I would partake with the guys.

"Derek, how many ice cubes would you like?" I heard Gene from the kitchen. "Two or three?" he would always say.

"Two please, Gene."

"Two it is!"

We would eat, have a drink, and then have conversation in the living room, exchanging stories.

My time with Rick and his family has been a very special part of my life. Gene passed away last year, and then Rick's mother Sherry passed shortly after. I miss them both dearly. Cheers to you, Gene, for your friendship is always in my pocket, and I always ask for "two" ice cubes when having a scotch!

Gene Sturm

"I've been working on some killer new riffs, check it out!" Rick screams over his penetrating guitar volume.

"Really—that loud? Dude, you have to turn it down, it's making me feel sick and it's killing my left ear!" I screamed back at Rick. I had this overwhelming feeling of way to much all at once. I didn't tell Rick I was feeling faint. He popped open a 40 oz. Schlitz malt liquor, his hands shaky.

"What's the matter, Rick?"

"Nothing," he said. "I haven't really had anything to drink today."

"Does having a beer help your hands not to shake?" I asked him.

"No, dumb ass!" he replied as he laughed. "I usually have two or three by this time of the day. But I am doing much better not drinking as much," Rick insisted.

On one hand, some of the thoughts were vaguely relevant: "Get the kids' Christmas presents," but then others imposed themselves for no apparent reason—"Don't spend any money"; "Avoid *habaneros*." Regardless, there was a kind of certitude to the process, as if it were all for the good, my brain doing a spot of rearranging with the most random inserts of meaningless information.

Yet I couldn't turn it off, or even trick it into stopping. "Think, think, think! Focus on a particular thing: baseball. A passionate encounter: April."

Okay, so those things would pop up, but the flood of other stuff still flowed by in the background, like a television droning on in the corner of the room.

I was twitchy, too, and wondered if Rick had noticed. I wanted to protest: "I'm not that damaged from the dive!" I said to Rick, just anxious to get on with ... something."

And my hands were all over the place: what was up with that? I caught my fingers frantically tapping on both legs as Rick plucked away.

I wanted to say something to Rick, but it didn't make sense to talk about things that didn't make sense, especially as this visit to his mangy joint was to say goodbye, not a cry for help.

The room seemed exceptionally bright, too, which seemed ridiculous, because the prairie house usually aspired to nothing more than semidarkness.

I shuffled about in the mess, looking for something to do. I poked at amplifiers and plucked guitar strings ... the keyboard; it was a Casio and looked like a big toy. It couldn't have been worth more than forty bucks. I had seen it before but never heard anyone play it—like really play it, although Rick can seemingly make noise on any instrument you put in his hands.

I'll make a bit of noise, I thought as I contemplated my repertoire, which consisted of chopsticks and, er, chopsticks.

I turned it on and pushed down on the keys. They felt strange, light and easy to the touch. One finger, two fingers, three fingers at once ... now a second hand.

I am playing.

I shifted in the seat and kept playing, not chopsticks or a riff or a tune, but a lengthy piece of music. I watched my hands perform and felt compelled not to take my focus away. Stopping at some midpoint didn't seem an option. I seemed propelled by a flow buried somewhere in the euphoria I was experiencing.

"What did you just do?" Rick said.

It sounded classical. I didn't know what it was. I didn't think it sounded familiar.

I knew it didn't make sense, but I didn't care. The noise in my head had kind of stopped. I wasn't twitchy.

Rick was tearing up. I couldn't stop smiling.

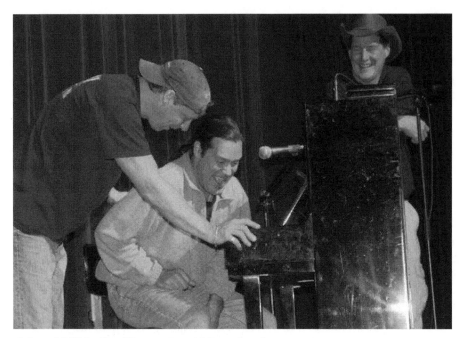

rick and bill, both with me when i hit my head

I continued to play as we both sat intensely tuned in to what my fingers were doing. It seemed not only weird, but almost surreal, begging for an explanation. This went on for another six hours, as I couldn't stop my mind from racing, and I certainly didn't want to stop playing. What if I stopped and couldn't do it again?

"It's 2:00 am," I said to Rick.

"Keep playing," he insisted.

"I'm tired, Rick, and my head is starting to hurt. I feel so anxious," I told him.

"C'mon, Derek, let's go, I will take you home." I turned off the keyboard as if I were saying a final goodbye to this sudden ability. "We can play all day tomorrow," Rick insisted.

"What the hell just happened, Rick?"

"It's warm in here," he said, between sobs, "really warm."

The radiator hummed gently in the corner.

SIX
Teenage Rampage

Fueled by a cocktail of prescription medication, weed and hormones, about the only thing teenage I did with the same dedication as baseball was chase girls.

By the time I had made it to the eighth grade, we had put together a large circle of very close friends. Even though we were typical kids when it came to getting in trouble, we never seemed to get caught. We weren't destructive kids, we preferred sneaking out for a late night gathering on our BMX bikes, or peeing off the bridge, or a get together at the local skating rink with a plan to skate doubles with a girl.

Most all of the guys in our group played competitive sports in school. It was common for coaches to split us up on different teams, as we seemingly had the edge on the other kids simply because we had already been playing a few years together.

My mother was commonly working two and three jobs at a time during my junior high school years, which would allow me plenty of hours to explore teenage promiscuity.

Tracy had become my first real girlfriend experience. She was of course one of the cutest girls at school. I would bounce down the hallways holding her hand, as the older boys would always give me that "She's dating you?" look, passing by us in the hallways. Tracy's family was incredibly nice to me every time I visited her house to see her. She grew up in the riverside area, just a mile from my neighborhood on the east side. Even though our boyfriend-girlfriend experience would be short-lived, Tracy would remain in my life to this very day.

During my last visit home to the Midwest (2011), I anxiously dialed Tracy's phone to catch up. She has been married to Jeff—whom I think the world of—for many years, and have two beautiful children.

"I'm not feeling so well today," she said over the phone. "Jeff is exhausted, back and forth to the hospital. The kids have been helping as much as they can, it's just overwhelming, Derek." Tracy's tired voice was something very hard to hear.

"Would it be all right if I went to the hospital with you? Maybe Jeff could take a break and get some stuff done around the house, or even just take a nap."

"That would be really nice," she affirmed with her soft and always kind tone. "I can give you a tour of the hospital, and they even have a piano," she said excitedly, as she was aware of my newfound ability. Tracy had never seen me play a piano, and under the circumstances, I wasn't sure if I could play, my emotions were just overwhelming me while there.

We walked through the floor saying hello to the passing nurses, Tracy introducing me as a childhood friend. I held her hand as we walked; it reminded me of junior high school.

"We have to get back," she said to me quietly. We made our way back to her room, and the nurse was finishing up preparation for Tracy's next few hours in the hospital.

"What is that?" I asked Tracy.

"17,000 dollars of poison," she answered.

I wasn't sure how to respond. I sat and stared at the bag of fluid they were about to pump into her fragile body, and it seemed like another one of those moments where time simply stood still.

She sat down quietly as the nurse hooked up an IV line.

"There you are, my dear," the nurse said.

"How long does this take?" I was curious as to this whole process.

"We will sit here for 4-5 hours now," she said. I pulled my chair up closer so we could be right next to each other. As she reached over, Tracy put her warm hand upon mine. "Thank you," she said.

"I'm so sorry you have to go through this," I told her. I was tearing up.

"I'm okay, Derek," she replied as she softly petted my hand.

There was a moment of peace that came over me while sitting with Tracy. A couple of tears ran down her face as I reached over to wipe away the presence of her pain.

"I'm with you, Tracy, and I will always love you and Jeff, and the kids."

The next few hours would provide me with a new appreciation for this terrible sickness we call cancer. I did end up playing that piano in the foyer before we left the hospital. Tracy sat next to me as Jeff stood right next to her. I was so nervous to show her this newfound talent.

"I can't believe you're playing the piano, Derek."

"Neither can I, Tracy."

We laughed and headed out, as we had now been at the hospital for several hours. I was emotionally exhausted.

As I logged into Facebook to check my e-mail, which had become our way of communicating the last couple of years, I was made aware of Tracy's passing. It was finally over. I took a breath and began to cry as I searched for her last e-mail to me. I just needed to read it again.

> *I am excited for your book to get to the stores so I can get a copy ... however, after it's out and you visit Sioux Falls again,*

I am coming for my autograph ... since November, I have had lots of minihills to climb, a lot of med changes, and they take me time to get used to ... but other than that, I work hard every day to get stronger and feel better ... they have reduced my chemo from three times a month for just twice a month for me.... I am loving having that extra time off!!!...hug those beautiful girls for me!! tracy

Tracy passed away July 27, 2013 at 5:00 pm.

"There's a party tonight," Curt said. It was the end of the day and the bell was getting ready to ring. We would gather the usual posse—Wayne, Curt, Jim, Kim, Mike, Bryan, Todd, Tommy, and a few more.

"What time is the keg party?" Jim screamed at Curt.

"Around eight tonight," Curt answered.

I had never really had an interest in alcohol growing up. This was my first keg party, and I knew I had to act like the older kids at the party, and try to look like I had done this sort of thing before. I mean c'mon, I'm in seventh grade, I can do this.

I can't remember how many beers I choked down, possibly eight. I do recall Curt attempting to get me home. "I can't take you to my house," Curt said. "My dad will kill us."

Curt was close to my mom. "Let's go to my house. Mom will be sleeping," I told Curt.

Somehow, Curt propped me on his handlebars. "Hang on," he insisted. I must have hung on, as we made it to my house, some two miles up the way.

The lights were still on. "Oh, shit!"I said, "Mom is awake." I was in no shape to be doing anything but going straight to bed. We walked in, and the beer smell on my breath obviously gave my mother a reason to ask where we had been, not to mention my warbling entrance.

"He doesn't feel so good," Curt said to my mom.

"What happened?" she asked.

"We drank beers at a party."

I needed to throw up now, as listening to the conversation between them was making me even more feeling sick. Curt rode his bike home. I made my way to the toilet with Mom's help, and began throwing up as I listened to my mother cry as she held me.

"I can't believe you did this, Derek." She continued to rub my head, assisting me into a deep sleep. It was a quiet morning the next day. I felt terrible for disappointing her.

I really didn't want junior high to end. High school seemed like it would be way too serious. How would I fit in? I am a cross between a jock and a pothead, and I bounced in between both groups of kids the entire time between seventh and twelfth grade.

Our last summer before entering high school would be spent as if we were never going to see one another again. Some of us would go to Lincoln High School, some would go to Washington, and some to O'Gorman High School. I was an east sider growing up, so I would continue on to Lincoln.

with Curt and Rick, no idea what we were up to here

High school would challenge me. I found the curriculum very intense. I suppose this would be from the last few years of simply not paying attention to schoolwork. By this time, my hair was a little past my shoulders (a mini mullet), and I had talked my mother into buying me a black leather jacket for Christmas.

My father had allowed me to pierce my ear the year prior, my present for getting good grades. I wanted to be like the older kids (Dave and Mike), who were playing in rock bands and had all the girls chasing them. I always looked up to Dave and Mike. Dave played the bass guitar and had long hair. Mike played guitar and also had long hair, but more than that, Mike could play "Eruption," the Eddie Van Halen famous guitar solo.

Mike went to a different junior high school than I, so I really never got to see Mike play. It was always hearsay. "He can play 'Eruption' by Van Halen," I heard someone say in the hallway one day. It was one of those always floating around comments about Mike. I wanted Dave's stage presence and Mike's "Eruption" playing fingers. Through high school, I would attend parties where Dave and Mike were playing, and this would become my rock and roll superstar stimulant. There was a short moment when I got to act like a rock star, as Rick, Curt, Dave, Mike, and I would eventually belt out a handful of eighties cover songs.

With a continually growing concern in her tone, Mom would ask, "How is school going?"

"It's all right," I would ensure. I was struggling with keeping up with homework due to my busy schedule with my friends. My grades began to dwindle, and my attitude was becoming more difficult for a single mother of two boys to deal with, all of which would lead me to a little stint with Mr. Nicholas, a high school teacher at Lincoln.

He was an older teacher, maybe in his later fifties. I would enter his classroom, sometimes tardy, and he would consistently harp on me. Although my behavior was increasingly challenging during my high school years, I was still a very liked kid by my friends and instructors. I walked in tardy this day, as we all snuck out to smoke some pot before going back to class.

"Go to the office, please, Derek," Mr. Nicholas said in a sharp tone.

I can't get in trouble again, my mind immediately thought. "I'm not going," I said as I made my way to my seat.

"You're tardy, you need a slip from the office, or I can call down and ask them to come and get you."

I knew my mother would be pissed off to hear of me getting in trouble again, as I was running out of chances at school. "I'm not going," I insisted again.

As he grabbed me by the arm, he began gently pushing me towards the door.

I reached and grabbed both of his arms, moving him aside. I didn't wildly start swinging angry fists around, rather just a slight adjustment as to where I thought he should be standing, and obviously not in my way. He buzzed down to the office in his nervous voice and requested they come and remove me from class. Mr. Hoff entered with a stern look. By this time, most of the kids were laughing and throwing out banter, somewhat encouraging me to challenge the teacher.

I had a really cool bond with Mr. Hoff. He was indeed my favorite principle. He had a special connection with many of us kids, and a certain way of handling us "on the edge" kids.

"Come with me, Derek," Mr. Hoff said. I followed him back to the office. We sat down for yet another chat in regard to my behavior. "You can't put your hands on a teacher, Derek, you know this." I looked down, as I knew I had disappointed him.

Mr. Hoff called my mother in for a meeting the next day.

"We are going to have to expel your son, Ms. Amato." This wasn't good. I knew what was coming next.

"I have had enough, Derek," my mother softly said to me. "I have called your father. You will be going to live with him for a while."

I was shattered. I loved the idea of going to dad's, but my mother was my best friend, and even though I was in need of some discipline, I couldn't imagine not having Mom next to me, and of course, I was worried as to what my brother would do without me.

I packed my stuff that following week and away I went, back to southern California. I never questioned my father's authority, so my grades during the rest of the school year at Katella High School were solid. I was moved up to the varsity baseball team with Katella, but I didn't get much playing time in, as most of the varsity boys were 6'4" and throwing in the upper eighties and lower nineties, and I, just an average sized kid from the Midwest, but my curve ball kept me in with the upper levels of talent.

Even though my trip to California led to exceptional grades that year, I became restless and talked Mom into letting me come home, and back to the Midwest I went. I wanted to desperately get back and show Mom some of the improvements I had made. I felt like I had made some headway with my attitude and outlook on the whole scenario, as Dad's stern presence did in fact make a difference. Now, looking back, I was just a pissed off high school kid who needed a father figure around, and the chances of that happening was pretty bleak.

That summer, I wandered over to Bryan's house one evening for a get together. I walked in to a cloud of smoke, black lights shining on Ozzy posters, and a few other high school kids I didn't know.

"Who's that girl?" I asked Bryan.

"That's my girlfriend," he said proudly.

"Really?" I was curious, of course. The music was blaring.

"Turn it down!" screamed Sally, Bryan's mom, from upstairs.

Bryan's mom was totally cool. I always thought highly of her and loved hanging out at their house, plus, Bryan's sisters, all three of them, were very pretty, but older than us. Passing around a bag of Doritos as we smoked pot and threw playful banter back and forth, I looked at Bryan and said, "I'm going to marry your girlfriend."

"That's funny," he replied. Two weeks later, I was dating my soon-to-be wife.

"Do you want to go to prom with me, Derek?" my new girlfriend asked.

I had never been to a high school prom, it just didn't seem appealing to me. "That would be fun," I answered, simply hoping to please her with my uneasy tone.

"I will pick you up around 5:00 pm," she said.

I was excited, as I had many friends who went to Brandon High School, and I was eager to show off my new girlfriend, or, I should say, I was eager to join her in front of her peers.

Donna arrived a bit late, dressed in the cutest sailor-looking type outfit. I just remember it being blue and white, and she looked hot, very hot.

"Have you been drinking?" I asked, as she seemed to be slurring upon her arrival.

"I have!" she answered, laughing. It wasn't looking good at this point.

"Are you able to go to the prom like that?"

"I don't think so," and now she was staggering to reaffirm she had consumed way too much alcohol.

"You better come in and sit down," my mom insisted.

The prom never happened for us that night. I ended up laying her on the couch in the living room for a much needed nap. A couple hours later, she popped up feeling much better.

"Thank you," she told me, "and I am so sorry for this."

"Don't worry about it, it was just a dance." We both wanted to show each other off, and I could tell she was sad we never got the opportunity to share high school prom together.

A few months passed. I was buzzing around like a little kid in a candy store. I was in love. "Let's move in together," she said one day while we were at the park.

"You haven't even graduated yet," I said, although a seemingly excited tone came from my mouth. I had been working at Minerva's Restaurant with Wayne at this time. We moved in to a small apartment on Minnesota Avenue shortly after. It would be a most challenging next six months, as acting like adults seemed to be a not so easy process.

"I have court in the morning," she told me before we went to sleep.

"For what?"

"Remember that car accident I told you about? It was a couple years back. My parents are meeting me at the courthouse. Will you drop me off and wait for me while I go in?"

"Of course," I said.

We pulled up to the courthouse. "Good luck," I said, leaning over to kiss her.

After forty-five minutes of waiting in the car, she finally came walking out of the courthouse with her parents. Her father was hugging her as she cried. "Oh, shit," I said to myself, "what the hell just happened in there?" My mind began racing. She looked sad and broken.

She opened the car door. "Hurry, go to the bank, fast."

"Now?"

"Hurry up!" she said, her voice shaking.

"Okay," I nervously told her. She didn't say much on our way over to the bank. I pulled up, and she almost jumped out even before the car stopped.

"I will be right back," she said, slamming the car door.

Once again, she came walking out of the bank with that broken look on her face. "What's going on?" She was crying frantically.

"It's all gone."

"What is?"

"They left not one penny in our bank account."

"What?" We had managed to stuff a few thousand dollars away, as Donna was working for a company selling cleaning products and making a fairly decent amount of money. We were planning to leave for California with what we had saved.

The people she got into a car accident with had sued her, and the judge froze the bank account during the court hearing. She was devastated, and I was pissed off that someone would take everything we had worked so hard to save up.

"I think we need to get out of this city," she said, "as soon as possible."

I agreed, and we began to pack our small apartment of only needed items we could fit into two boxes. The rest was sold in a garage sale.

"We should drive out to California," I told her. "Let's sell the old car and get a different one." I found a little red sports car that day in the newspaper. "I'm going to test drive that car," I told her on the phone that afternoon. She was still working when I left the apartment.

Walking up to the house that had the car for sale gave me a few moments to get excited about ownership of this fine used machine. The gentleman gave me the typical walk around.

"It's in pretty good shape," he said, reassuring the investment we were about to make. "Go ahead, take it out for a while," he told me. Buying it or not, I really wanted to take this car out for a drive.

"Perfect," I responded, "I will see you in a while."

"Take your time," he insisted. I must have been gone a bit longer than he expected, I'm guessing maybe an hour had passed, as I was buzzing around town. Why are those police cars pulling up to me so quickly? I was parked in the parking lot of a sports store, trying to mess with getting the stereo to work.

"Put your hands outside the windows!" one of the police officers hollered at me.

"What? What is happening?" came screaming from my mouth, almost in a vocal attempt to let the officers know I wasn't scared. Actually, I was so scared I couldn't really even respond.

"Put your hands outside the window!" a second voice screamed at me.

"Don't shoot me!" I yelled, putting my hands outside the window as requested.

Five police cars suddenly surrounded me, and it all happened so fast that I didn't even have time to even guess what was happening. They had drawn their guns and were pointing them directly at my head. I thought I was going to throw up at one point. Even though this only lasted 45 seconds, it seemed like 45 minutes.

I felt firm hands grab my wrists, tightly. They began pulling me straight out of the window on to the ground with my face directly planted in the pavement. I felt a foot on the back of my head, pushing my face even harder against the concrete. The only thing I could think of to say was, "My parents are cops," and it did not make one bit of difference, as I thought to myself, *This get-out-of-jail card is a hoax.*

I was handcuffed and taken to jail. I kept asking what the hell was going on, and even though I was read my rights, I had no explanation given to me as to what had just transpired. I thought maybe I had a warrant I was unaware of.

Walking into the jail holding area was eerie. I was familiar with this place, not because of getting in trouble, but my mother worked at the sheriff's department growing up, not to mention my father was a police officer in California, and my grandfather chief of police.

"You have been arrested for auto theft, Mr. Amato." I was handcuffed to a cold steel bench.

"What do you mean?" I asked?

"You stole a vehicle from a private owner and he called it in, saying you also had a gun."

"A gun? Stolen? I was just test driving the car," I insisted. The gentleman who sat next to me on the bench was also handcuffed.

"What ya in for?" he asked.

"Auto theft I guess," I responded.

"Oh, man, that's big time, you're going away for a long time," he ensured me. Now I was nervous.

A couple hours passed as I sat quietly handcuffed to that cold bench. The owner of the car finally walks in and tells the police officer that there was a misunderstanding. He thought I was going on a test drive for ten minutes, not an hour. When he called in the car as stolen, the officers were instructed that that car thief may be on the run, which apparently sounded just like "He may have a gun." I was released, and I walked out with the guy that I almost bought a car from.

I called Donna. "Hey, you're never going to believe this."

"Where have you been?" she asked.

"Well, that car I took for a test drive—you know, the little red one?"

"Ya."

"They thought I stole it, so they arrested me and pointed guns to my head."

"Are you serious?" she said, almost as if she didn't believe me.

"I will tell you all about it when you get home."

"Are you okay?"

"Ya, it was pretty scary, I've never had a gun pointed at me."

Donna got home from work later that evening. We laughed about the whole car theft thing as we continued gathering scattered items that needed to come with us—a baseball glove, some old photos, clothes....

A few days passed, we were eager to hit the road. "We aren't going to have enough money to buy a different car, this old car just isn't worth much," she said. We sold the car for a couple hundred bucks. The car needed to go away anyways, as it had bad memories attached to it. It was the same car she had gotten into the accident with, which led to the freezing of the bank account money we had desperately relied on to start our new lives with.

It's time to go. We finished packing, and I picked up two Greyhound bus tickets to California.

Jumping on a Greyhound bus at the time seemed like we were going on some kind of guided tour, as we passed cornfields that went for miles, and beautiful mountains through Utah that looked more orange in color than the typical brown dirt we were used to seeing. It was fun to just sit back, talk amongst ourselves, eat snacks, and occasionally prop our heads upon each other's shoulders for naps in between miles.

After a day of travel, it was starting to become uncomfortable sitting for such long periods. I was getting grumpy, she was getting impatient.

"What's that hitting my seat?" she asked me.

"What do you mean?"

"Shhhh," she quieted me. "Listen, can you hear that tapping? It's hitting the back of my seat," she whispered to me.

"What is?"

"I'm not sure. I think someone behind us is kicking the seat."

I slowly leaned over, just enough to where I could peek through the separated seats. "Oh, god, he's got a knife!"

"What do you mean he's got a knife?"

"The guy behind us," I said as quietly as I could.

A few miles back, the bus had stopped at a small town and picked up two new passengers. Of course, they decided to sit right behind us. The gentleman was cussing out loud and had a knife, which he was poking into the back of Donna's seat, and saying he was going to kill the bus driver to his partner.

"We have to move at the next stop," I insisted.

Over the loudspeaker came a firm voice. "Anyone using marijuana on my bus will be kicked out. I am not playing games here, folks." I could smell pot smoke, and guess what, right behind us, the two new passengers were smoking a joint as if it were no big deal.

"Put it out!" one guy said to his partner, "he's going to kick us off in the middle of nowhere."

"Screw him, I will kill this bus driver and I will drive this damn bus!" he stated.

At this point, Donna and I thought for sure we were going to be killed on our new journey seeking California sunshine. The knife stabbing into her seat came to a halt.

"They are sleeping," I told her. "Let's change seats when we stop in Vegas." We did.

We walked into the bus depot in Vegas as if we just discovered the most miraculous place on earth.

"Look at all the lights! The people are everywhere, and even prostitutes." It was so exciting to see, an unfamiliar whole other world to the both of us. Donna sat staring at a man sitting at the slot machines. He was intoxicated, aggressively cussing at the machine as if it owed him his money back.

Suddenly, the man looked directly at Donna, asking her what her problem was.

"Don't respond," I told her. I wasn't scared of much at the age of eighteen. I walked over to the man and told him to watch his mouth when talking to my girlfriend. Well, that didn't go so well, as he now was cussing me up and down, which became my first experience being referred to as a cracker. The security officer came over and escorted the old fella out the door. "You can't stare at people," I told Donna, "you're going to get me in a fight."

We got back on the bus.

"Just a few more hours and we're there," I told her. It was now early morning, somewhere around 3:00 am.

Fresh off the bus, we had two boxes of 'stuff' and $75.00 between us.

"Who's picking us up?"

SEVEN
Show and Tell

I knew this was beyond strange, but it had happened, hadn't it?

During a mostly sleepless night, I felt like I wanted to shout from the rooftops, but knew I should move cautiously. Even telling my family would be weird. It seemed like an idea from a children's cartoon—man hits head and becomes something he wasn't previously. I closed my eyes as my nervous hands searched for a spot to rest on my chest.

Nevertheless, I knew I couldn't hold onto the secret. I'd start with Mom; perhaps I should show, rather than tell her? "We should go over to the music store this morning," I said, getting another cup of coffee.

By breakfast, I was like a little kid trying to keep the lid on something, and Mom kept asking me why I wanted her to drive to the music store with me, but eventually relented. "I want to show you something."

"Are you planning on buying something?" Mom curiously asked.

"No, I just thought you should see something really cool." My fingers were continually tapping on my knee; I assumed it was simply a nervous or excited reaction on our way to the music store.

On arrival, I darted over to a digital piano. "You want to buy a piano, son?" I was looking for a button that would turn the machine on.

"Here, sit next to me," I told Mom.

"Can I help you?" a voice behind me asks.

"Oh, no, thank you, I am just looking. How do you turn this machine on?" I asked him.

He reached over and clicked the on button. "There you are."

I was seemingly uncomfortable with the salesman hanging over me, so I responded with a "Thank you, I'm just going to play this for a minute," in hopes of making him wander off.

I was shaky with nerves as I looked down to the unfamiliar, although inviting black and white keys. *Geeeez, I sure hope this still works*, I thought. It did, with the same flourish and fluidity as the night before, the images of the keys immediately sharpening in my mind as I slipped away for a moment into my own little lost space. I even swayed the exact same way that day as I do today when I play the piano, very Stevie Wonderish kind of movement!

at Backbone Recording Studio for filming Ingenious Minds

My mother's demeanor went immediately into that shock and awe mode, as she attempted to ask, "How?" "But, when...." I looked over to my mother, almost as if I was waiting for approval, and the tears in her eyes were enough to ensure me something very special had taken place.

"Don't cry, Mom, I feel good today." Now, my eyes were beginning to tear up; no one likes seeing their mother cry.

"I'm not sad, son," she affirmed.

I continued playing as if I were Beethoven, eyes closed, smiling, and how ironic, half deaf.

"How long ya been playing, young man?" I figured the salesman would make his way around sooner or later.

I looked at him and responded, "About seven hours, Sir."

"No, I mean how long have you played the piano?" he repeated.

"About seven hours, Sir." This time, it looked like he simply thought I was being a smart ass. I reached over and turned off the piano. "Thank you, have a good day," I told the salesman as we made our way out. Mom was beside herself at this point, and I certainly wasn't sure of the response I would get during the drive home, as these types of things don't pop up in ones life often.

The drive back home was quiet; both Mom and I were rattled. I couldn't explain it. I told her: "It just happened at Rick's last night." My mother's Christianity has always been present in our lives. It was easy to know that her thoughts on this would be put in the "This is God's work" category.

I was now overly excited to get going back to Colorado. But wait, what am I suppose to do with this? The pace of my racing mind began to make me feel as if I were on overload. *Scrambled* is more like it. The spots I am seeing are everywhere, but seemingly in a pattern. These particular patterns would later become vivid black and white squares in constant motion, described to me by Dr. Andrew Reeves of the Mayo Clinic as yet another rare condition called *synesthesia*. But, at that moment, they seemed like garbled moving patterns that just wouldn't stop.

After dinner, I went back in the bedroom to finish packing stuff. I grabbed the phone while pacing between rooms stuffing clothes into my travel bag.

"Hey, what are you doing?"

"Not much. How are you?" Jason asked. "Where are you?"

"I'm good, getting stuff ready to head back to Denver. I'm still at Mom's in Sioux Falls. Jason always has the most infectious and positive delivery when calling.

Jason and I worked together in the telecom industry as corporate trainers. We have always had a very sincere friendship since meeting, and his motivated and caring spirit has always fascinated me. His energy lights up a room like no other, and he is just one of those amazing people you want in your life; actually, he is one of those people we all need in our lives.

with jason drenner in new york city

"Do you have a minute?"

"Absolutely. I just got in from traveling." Jason is always traveling for work.

"I have to tell you about the craziest thing that happened last week. "

"Well, tell me," he said. I was sure he was expecting an "I saw the prettiest girl out last night" kind of comment to come out of my mouth.

"I had an accident," I told him.

"What? What do you mean an accident?"

"I hit my head when I dove into the swimming pool."

"Did you hurt yourself?" Jason's tone became more empathic.

"My hearing is muffled in my left ear, and I am getting these headaches that are brutal."

"How are you feeling now?"

"I'm still a little sore, but getting there. Things are just kind of fuzzy."

"What do you mean fuzzy?"

"Like not making complete sense, and my mind is racing nonstop. I still can't remember how I got to my mother's house. I thought I was in spring training for baseball in Arizona." He laughed.

"Maybe you should take a few weeks to relax."

"Relax? I have to get back and find a damn job."

"Job hunting is the worst. When are you going back to Denver?"

"Probably in a couple days, finishing up packing and I am ready to go. I have to visit Wayne before I go."

I've always had the same exact process when visiting back home. I go directly to Wayne's house, then Rick's, and then the YMCA for a workout, which would turn into more of a two-hour trot around the facility to say hello to anyone and everyone.

"Oh, hey, I wanted to share one more thing before I let you go."

"What's that, Bro?"

"When I woke up a few days after my accident, I could play the piano."

"You really did hit your head, you're nuttier than squirrel shit (Jason's favorite saying)," he replied, still laughing.

"I know. Right."

"Are you pulling my chain, Bro?"

I was now laughing, as the playful tone in our conversation switched immediately to "Tell me more now."

"What the hell are you saying? You just sat down and played? I didn't even know you ever played the piano."

"I don't," I insisted. "Wait—I do now, but I never had prior."

"This is the craziest thing I have ever heard. C'mon, Derek, you're screwing with me. Have you told anyone else yet?"

"I told my mother this morning. I took her to the music store and showed her."

"What did she say?"

"Nothing. She sat and cried."

I hung up, still wanting to tell Jason more of this bizarre finding, but I knew I had to get going; my children were on my mind, and I was adamant about making the long trek home to Colorado. One more stop and I am out of here. I had to not only give Wayne his goodbye hug, but Norm worked up the street from Rick's house.

"Hey, Wayne, can you meet me at Rick's before I head out of town?"

"Ya, what time?"

"Like an hour. I'm running over to see Norm," who we often referred to as "The Bail," short for Bailey, of course.

"Okay, see you in an hour."

Walking into the gas station to see Norm always got me so excited, as he never expected me, so it's a big surprise. I had a baseball cap on, my eyes still black and blue from the diving accident. I looked down as I entered so he couldn't see my face.

"Can I help you?" he said.

"Um, ya," and I started to make my way to the back of the counter, still looking down, not making eye contact. I could tell he was nervous that I was entering the cashier area, and I was guessing he thought he was about to get robbed.

I looked up, and Norm immediately had the biggest smile on his face, giving me his signature "You little shit!" as I hugged him like I didn't want to let go. My love for this man is beyond explanation.

After a few moments of catching up, he ordered me to go and pick out some candy. This was another consistent thing with Norm since childhood. "Grab something for the road," he said, so I did.

"I wanted to see you before leaving for Colorado. I also wanted to show you something, but since you're working and there is no piano in the gas station, I will have to tell you rather than show you." His eyes widened as I explained the piano situation. I could feel his excitement, curiosity, and even a small amount of thinking I was pulling his leg.

"You little shit!" he said again, almost as if I were telling a made-up story.

"I love ya, Norm, see you next time. Thought I'd tell ya!"

EIGHT
CALIFORNIA DREAMING

Being athletic, attractive, and spirited counts for something when you're starting your journey into adult life, but in California, it's hard to stand out in the pack. I had no intentions of furthering my education, as college seemed financially challenging without a baseball scholarship.

Accepting the fact that my baseball playing days had come to an end was a frustrating process. Although the shoulder damage from every one of those pitching practice days and thousands of curve balls had simply taken its toll (thanks, Don), and it seemed easier to blame the injury rather than not having the ability to possibly play pro ball, either way, I would find coaching to soon replace that baseball void.

California has a much different pace than the Midwest. There is that special energy, or maybe it's just that everyone around me seems to be chasing dreams out here. Everyone wants to be an actor, or a rock star, or just simply attached to one.

where dreams are made

It was 1986, and big hair, glam bands, ripped jeans, and aqua net hairspray scented the room of every party. Although I was smoking pot, I really didn't have a desire to partake in other drugs, and, at that time, cocaine seemed to be the drug of choice for many. I tried it, but it wasn't for me.

"I'm running to the grocery store," I told Donna.

"Here, I made a list for you."

We were staying with my mother in Santa Anna, in a apartment complex called the Californians. I jumped in the car and headed out. I grabbed some milk and other random items listed. As I was waiting in line reviewing the list—as there is always that one item you think you are forgetting when at the grocery store,

"What did you forget?" a voice from behind me asked.

"Pardon me?"

"Looks like you can't find something on that list you're looking at."

"I think I got it all."

"I'm Steve," he said, reaching out to shake my hand, "Parker," he adds, sounding very proud of his last name.

"Steve PARKER, nice to meet you. I'm Derek."

"What do you do?" he asked me.

"I just moved here, I haven't found a job yet."

"You're in luck, I need a roofer immediately."

"A roofer? I have never roofed a house in my life," I said, chuckling.

"Don't worry about it, I will teach you. Here, this is my number, call me tomorrow and I will get you started." I headed back to our apartment, excited to tell Donna about finding a job.

I threw the keys on the counter. "I just met Steve."

"Who?"

"Steve PARKER," I repeated, annunciating his last name just as he had. "He wants me to start roofing houses tomorrow."

"Do you know how to do that stuff?"

"Nope, not a clue. He said he would teach me. It doesn't sound that difficult to learn," I ensured.

The next morning, I sprung out of bed early. "Where is that piece of paper with Parker's number on it?" I woke Donna. "Hey, did you see that paper with a phone number on it?"

"No, did you throw it away?"

"I don't think so." I continued to scour the apartment. It's got to be somewhere. I found it. I had placed it in the bag of groceries and threw it in the trash.

"Good morning, Mr. Parker, this is Derek, we met at the store yesterday. Do you still want me to work?"

"Can you be ready in an hour, Derek?"

"What should I wear?"

"Old jeans, if you have some," Parker responded. "Do you have gloves?"

"I don't."

"I will bring you a pair."

"Okay, great, see you in an hour.

I put on a pair of jeans and a t-shirt. "Can I wear a baseball cap to work on my first day?" Donna was now up and getting breakfast made.

"I think it's okay to wear a baseball cap," she ensured me. I heard a horn outside, and the rumble of his big, white truck with a bunch of supplies in it.

"Gotta go!" I said, running out the door. Love you, honey." Donna kissed me goodbye.

"Good morning, Mr. Parker."

"Call me Steve, Are you ready to be a roofer?"

"I am."

The drive took us about 45 minutes. There is this specific smell to California mornings. "Why does it smell like oranges?" I asked Parker.

"That's an orange grove," he replied as he pointed.

"Ah, makes sense!" I said, laughing.

We pulled up to a large house.

"There she is," Steve says.

"Who is she?" I asked.

"The house," Steve says, laughing. "Grab all of the tools, belts, shingles, and anything else in the back of the truck, and put it all on the other side of the house."

"Okay," I said, a little curious.

"I will be right back."

Steve went into the house to talk to the house owner. I loaded all the tools out of the truck as instructed and carried them over to the side of the house.

"All right, here we go," Steve said in a cheerful voice, like he was really happy to have someone to work with. "Here, grab this bucket and take it with you up the ladder."

I climbed the ladder cautiously, as holding the bucket filled with tools only allowed me one hand on the ladder. I made it. It seemed like I was ten stories high. Steve followed me on the ladder carrying the tool belts.

It was getting warm already. The pitch on the roof was beginning to hurt my ankles and knees within the first hour. Sports beat the heck out of my knees growing up.

"You see that house?" Steve asked me.

"The big house?"

"Yes, the big house. That is where they filmed *Ferris Buehler's Day Off.*"

"That's really cool."

"Here, stand behind me and hand me the shingles."

Like a quarterback, I stood behind Steve, feeding him shingles between his legs as he nailed them in place.

After six hours of this process, my ankles were begging to get off the roof already.

"Here, Derek, take my Zacto knife and trim the shingles where I have them marked."

"Cut them?" I asked.

"Yes, cut along the mark and we can finish this row." The cedar shingles smelled strong, or fresh may be a bit more appropriate.

"Here you go," I said as I handed the stack of cut shingles back to Steve.

The day was going great. The sun was out, and I was feeling good about my new job. "Here you go," as I handed Steve back his Zacto knife.

"Thanks," he said, stuffing it in his back pocket.

"All right, just like we did the last batch!" Steve barked out. Back to the quarterback position, and handing him shingles as fast as he can nail them down.

"That's it," commented Steve as he stood up from his leaning over position. I was still directly behind him.

"Ouch!" I reached down to feel where my stomach had been poked. "Steve, I'm bleeding pretty badly!"

"What?" Steve looked down to see blood running down the side of my jeans. I pulled my shirt up.

"That's not good," I told Steve. I covered the bleeding area with my palm and started swaying. Steve grabbed me. I was getting dizzy. Steve sat me down.

"Hold this on your stomach, I'm going to get you down the ladder."

When Steve stood up, the Zacto knife in his back pocket had sliced a perfectly straight three-inch gash in my stomach.

He had run into the house and gotten some gauze and tape to cover the cut. We ended up pushing the fat and muscle back into the three-inch gash. After a few minutes of bandaging, we loaded up the truck and he dropped me off back at home. My roofing career was short-lived, as Steve didn't have enough work to keep me full time, although we were able to save up enough money to move into our own little apartment.

I really enjoyed my time with Steve PARKER. He offered me a job at a time of need, and he was absolutely a nice, genuine guy. Each day I see this scar on my stomach, it reminds me of the Ferris Buehler house.

The initial excitement of doing it 'on our own' faded quickly. I was anchorless: no mother's guidance, no Norm Bailey; even baseball was becoming a memory.

Donna struggled to cope, and our once dynamic chemistry collapsed into a volatile relationship, and the physical and emotional abuse I was about to encounter would haunt me for many years following.

At nineteen, I was starting to think I had taken on more than I could handle. Work was irregular, my relationship rocky, and the dreams of being successful in California were quickly beginning to fade.

I picked up work here and there, a hospital, at a lumberyard … anywhere, but it was hard to get ahead.

I eventually picked up a full time and more challenging job with a pressure washing equipment distributor, Chemex Western. It was a real business, something I felt I could learn and with a trickle of income providing a hint of stability, which would reaffirm our commitment to each other and push forward.

My direct boss at Chemex was Michael. Michael was a healthy-sized guy, early thirties, and had a very enthusiastic and happy demeanor. Michael spent much time training me in the different areas—fixing pressure washers, mixing chemicals, and typical warehouse duties. Chemex Western was owned by the Bagwell family. Gary, the owner, was a most inviting personality, although firm, but I loved how he treated his sons David and Chuck at work. Gary left a very strong impression with me, and I have always considered myself very lucky for the opportunity he gave me, not to mention his family treating me wonderfully as a friend and employee.

My favorite memory of working at Chemex, well, I shouldn't say *favorite*, possibly funniest, story is a bit more fitting. I was driving the service truck to repair a pressure washer at the Coca Cola facility in Los Angeles. I had gotten lost on my way there and somehow ended up in Compton.

Compton has a pretty bad reputation and is a very tough neighborhood. I pulled over at a liquor store, as I was getting nervous that I was late for the service call. Eileen answered the phone. "Can I speak to Gary real quick, Eileen, I'm lost and need directions."

"Hey, Derek," Gary said, cheerfully greeting me, "where are you?"

"I wouldn't be calling if I knew where I was, Gary."

"No, I mean what cross streets are you near?" I had pulled the service truck into the parking lot next to the liquor store. The pay phone was actually only 15 feet from the truck.

I told Gary the cross streets. "Hold on, let me grab a map."

I had my shirt off while driving, as it was really hot, and there was no air conditioning in the service truck. Just so you understand this moment, let me clarify. A white kid, no shirt on, was standing at a pay phone in the middle of Compton. *Something just doesn't jive with this whole moment*, I kept thinking to myself as I stood there holding the phone waiting for Gary to get the map.

"Okay, Derek, take blah blah blah, and you should get there in twenty minutes."

"Oh, shit, Gary!"

"What?"

"Hold on...." As I looked over my shoulder, I noticed two Hispanic men sitting in the service truck. They weren't actually just sitting, they were frantically trying to get the truck started, trying to steal the truck right in front of me.

The concrete parking strip was the only thing between the truck and the busy intersection. I ran towards the truck. "Hey!" I screamed, not quite sure how to react. I was scared to death, but I was even more scared to get back on the phone with Gary telling me I was fired.

I reached in the driver side window. I had no idea what I was trying to grab, so I grabbed the driver by the hair and I hung on for dear life. The truck did an almost jumping forward blast; the concrete barrier was just high enough to act as a small ramp. The truck sped into the middle of the busy intersection. Let me once again reflect: a white kid, no shirt on, middle of Compton, staring at a pay phone hanging there in wait, with a handful of hair in my right hand.

"Oh, god, Gary, this isn't good!"

"What happened, Derek?"

"Well, when I got out of the truck to call you, I was so nervous that I was late that I forgot to lock the truck when I got out to make a call."

"What?" Gary's voice was now intense.

"I was only 15 feet from the truck."

"Where are the keys?" Gary asked.

"Shit, I think I left them in the ignition!"

"I am sending David to pick you up," Gary instructed with a firm delivery in his voice.

I stood on the streets of Compton without a shirt on for 45 minutes. David pulled up. It was a quiet ride back, until David looked over at me and started busting up laughing. They took your shirt, too? I officially got my first spanking at work. Gary did not fire me. The truck was found like seven days later, stripped, and I mean stripped, yep, even the 10-dollar stereo Michael had put in to appease my complaining to not having music in the truck.

Shortly after my carjacking experience, I was once again in a trying position while working for Chemex. As I pulled into south central Los Angeles for a typical service call, I found myself lost again. We didn't have GPS! I got out of the truck, grabbed my keys this time, and began walking towards a convenient store to get directions.

"Hey, white boy!" a voice from behind me said, a young voice. I turn around and I was approached by a ten-year-old kid. "You want some crack, whitey?"

I was thinking, *What? What the hell kind of question is that coming from a kid?* I said, "You know, if I had more time, I would probably put you over my knee and give you a spanking."

Okay, maybe that wasn't the appropriate way to respond. "What did you say, cracker?" I was now being questioned and interrogated by a little kid with this huge afro, in the middle of the street.

"Forget it," I said and I turned to walk off.

"Hey!" he screamed. I looked back. This ten-year-old kid was now pointing a black pistol in my face.

I thought for a second that my life was done. That puking sensation quickly flooded my entire being. It was weird, almost like time had stood still, again. He put the gun in his jeans. I walked away praying every step, "Please don't shoot me in the back." I went on the service call, and never did see that kid again.

Pulling back in to the shop, I saw Michael in the back taking inventory. "Hey, Derek, how did it go?"

"Don't even ask," I told Michael.

"Why, did you get lost or have a problem with their machine?"

"Dude, I almost got my face blown off by a ten-year-old kid with a very big afro who called me whitey and cracker."

"Are you kidding me?"

"Do I look like I'm kidding, Michael?"

"Did you call the police?"

"No, I just wanted to get the hell out of there, man."

"Well, at least he didn't steal your truck."

"I'm going home early today, Michael."

My total focus on building a family was required when Donna fell pregnant. This was the most exciting news that I could possibly hear, but what am I going to tell Dad? Being the intense old-fashioned Catholic Italian man my father was would only make me wonder how I was going to share the news. We married in a courthouse ceremony in the presence of my father and his wife, Mary. Alex was born four months later, just three days before my birthday. Alex would become the joy of my life.

with kim and rick roach for alex's babtism

The new baby brought fresh responsibility and pressures on both of us. My career and creative ambitions in tatters slumped into depression, a condition fueled by my ongoing reliance on pain medication.

At the ripe age of twenty-one, it was time for Donna and I to take a step back and concede the real world wasn't quite ripe for conquering.

It was back to South Dakota.

NINE
Stepping On Stage

In the first few weeks after the accident, the urge to play piano pretty much all the time was overwhelming.

I told a few close friends and family members what had happened at Rick's but largely kept it to myself, as I didn't want to appear foolish or dishonest. I also feared that as soon as word spread, the talent would leave me: I had been burned by speaking too soon and enthusiastically about 'opportunities' before and couldn't abide the prospect of ridicule over something so personal.

Spending much of my time researching possible options and explanations for this magical experience, I stumbled upon the writings of Dr. Darold Treffert of the Wisconsin Medical Society, only to find out that he was the advisor for the film *Rainman*. My imagination was running wild with information overload from Dr. Treffert's work in defining "the savant."

This would become the beginning of a long road in my attempt to understand the different possibilities of what just may have happened to me. My conversations with Dr. Treffert continue today, as he has become a prominent voice in helping me understand this beautiful journey.

It would be almost a year later following my accident that my phone would ring with Kenny screaming, "Dude, we have to talk—NOW!"

Kenny and I lived in the same neighborhood just fifteen minutes west of Ft. Collins. I didn't care to live in the city as it was just way too busy. Jennifer and I had found a rental when I came back to Colorado after my accident. It was perfect, and we shared a large mountain home with our new roomies Josh and Dan.

My phone rang once again twenty minutes later; it was early afternoon now as I got ready to go for a hike with Murfee, our charming and full of life cairn terrier. I missed the call and decided to check my voice mail before running out the door with Murfee. Again, it was Kenny, and this time I could hear urgency in his message, so I immediately called him back, thinking something was wrong.

"Hey, Kenny, what ya up to?"

"Trying to get the boat fixed so we can go out fishing later. Are you up for it?"

"Of course! Let's take a few rods out this time. We can fish for both walleye and bass."

"Absolutely! Oh, how about playing with Stanley Jordan next month?"

"What are you talking about, Kenny?"

"I will tell you all about it when you get here." I wanted to know more that very moment; now my mind was racing with excitement.

"You mean Stanley, the jazz guitar god that Johnny Carson found playing on the subway?"

"Ya, that guy," Kenny laughed while responding.

"Oh, my god, hurry up and get the boat fixed! We can fish and talk about this some more."

"Are you sure it's the real Stanley Jordan?"

"Derek, I just hung up with Tippitina's in New Orleans. Remember, I lived there for years?"

"Oh, that's right, but I didn't know you knew Stanley."

"I don't. I know a few people that know a few people that know the general manager at the club. C'mon over."

I could hear him trying to crank the motor in the background. I scrambled about the house grabbing my fishing rod, cowboy hat, and a bottle of water.

Pulling up to Kenny's house, I saw DeeDee standing on the deck with the dogs waving me hello. "Hey, Dee, where's Kenny?"

"Hi, darlin', he's under the boat working on the motor." DeeDee has this lovely Southern drawl and this most inviting smile, and always welcomes me with a huge Southern hospitality hug.

"Dude, your hands are beat up," I told Kenny as I approached him still working on the boat. Ken has working man hands—short stubby fingers, calloused, cut up, dirt under his fingernails, the whole nine yards. He crawled out from under the boat motor.

"Hey, buddy," came his always consistent verbal welcome to me, as he leans over to hug me.

"Don't touch me with those dirty hands, Kenny!" He hugs me anyways.

"Let's go!" he says with great energy in his voice.

"Is it running?"

"Hell, yes, it's running!" Kenny can fix most anything that can be broken. Seriously, the guy is a master of tinkering with stuff; even if it doesn't need to be fixed, he's fixing it regardless. As we hook up the boat to the truck and throw our fishing rods in, DeeDee comes walking down the steps to remind us not to be late, as she was planning a dinner for later that evening, and this Southern girl can cook.

"Don't worry, honey," Kenny says to her smiling, "we're never late."

"Ya. right!" and she gives us that typical eye roll.

"I still think your wife is hot, Kenny." He gets this magical glow to him when I tease him about how pretty DeeDee is.

"She is, isn't she, and she's all mine!" We jump in the truck and head to the water, which is literally right around the corner.

After getting out on the water, we find a cozy little bay, drop anchor, and throw our lines out. "Okay, so here's the deal, Derek. We are leaving for New Orleans October 26th. It's not a huge paying gig, but I thought this would be something you would certainly want to do."

"How long do I have to play? What kind of piano will I get to play? Who's the sound guy? Where…?"

"Hold on, let me explain." Kenny went on to tell me how special this venue was, as everyone who is anyone has played there. I was getting more nervous with each sentence that came out of his mouth.

"I got one!" he screamed.

"Why do you always catch the first fish, bro?"

"It's all in the technique," he assures me, laughing as he reels in the first walleye of the day.

"That's bullshit, Kenny, what are you putting on your hook, something different than mine?"

"Just a worm." Kenny now holding his walleye in the air to rub it in. It's always a fishing derby when we are on the water, fierce competition amongst two men jumping around in a boat like two little kids.

fishing the world famous arkansas river in coloardo

"Anyways," he continues, "you will open the show for Stanley Jordan, can you believe it?"

"How long do I get to play?"

"You have forty minutes, Derek, so make every one of 'em count."

"Geeez, Ken, all of this makes me a little nervous. I never imagined something like this would ever happen, and I am a huge fan of Stanley. Will I get to hang out with him? Where will we stay? How much will I get paid? Do I get a baby grand to play on?

I had so many questions that I almost forgot I was fishing. "I think I got bite. Yep, it's a big one, bro!" I started to reel in my huge fish, Kenny telling me not to stress the line. "I got this one. Sonofabitch, I'm caught up in the motor, hold this," I said, handing Kenny my fishing pole.

"You don't have a fish on, you have a snag!" Kenny hollers, "take your pole, Derek, I have one on!" Sure enough, it's now Kenny 2,

Derek 0. We continued to discuss the Stanley gig for the next several hours on the water, Kenny answering my curious questions one after the other. He knew how excited I was to have this once in a lifetime opportunity.

"Hey, what time is it?" I chirped. "Great, its 8:00 pm, DeeDee is going to kill us." We have a bad habit of letting time slip right by when out fishing. "Call her and let her know we're running late, Ken."

"I didn't bring my phone," he said, raising his eyebrows, knowing we were in big trouble.

"I'm starving, let's head back." We arrived back to the house a bit after 9:00 pm. There she was standing on the deck, this time no happy welcoming wave as I usually get.

"Kenny, you could have called," she greeted us in a scolding tone.

"I left my phone, honey," delivering his excuse softly with tail between legs.

DeeDee gives me a hug, "Dinner is on the table, darlin'. Kenny, you're in the doghouse, babe," pointing at him, all with a tiny smile hidden behind her firm scowl at Ken.

I usually laugh and make light of our tardy habits, and DeeDee usually accepts my playful banter as more of an "I'm sorry, Dee, we won't be late again."

"Ya, right," she says to me, laughing.

We are staying with Paul while there, Derek."

"Who's Paul?"

"My brother, you ding a ling."

We arrived in New Orleans October 26th, just as planned. Paul welcomed us with open arms, his beautiful home, and surprised us with a dinner that was out of this world, and I mean serious cajun food! We had to go out the next day in search of a piano to rent, as this was my first experience with trying to collect the musical items needed for my performance. Thank god for Paul's help. He connected us with some people who took care of everything for me. Although it was a long day of running around in hot, humid weather, we made it back to the house in time for yet another amazing meal.

The next morning, I made an appearance at Tulane College. We toured the facility, met a bunch of really nice college kids, autographed photos—okay, I have to admit, this was my first experience autographing anything, and I must say it's a different feeling for sure. We then made our way to the college campus radio station for an in studio interview, and this would also be my first experience having one of my songs actually played on the radio. That, too, excited me very much.

The whole day was simply like a dream to me—meeting new faces, signing stuff, and just being treated so nicely by every single person I met, certainly a highlight I will always keep with me. The next morning, I was taken to visit the venue. I could see the big letters on the building as we approached.

"There it is," says Kenny proudly, "we're here. The famous Tippitina's!"

"I'm feeling a little sick, Ken, can we just sit here in the car for a few minutes?"

"Of course, Derek, are you all right?"

"I'm fine Ken, it's just all a little overwhelming." I started to tear up for no other reason than, "Is this really happening?" and I'm not sure if I am really even here.

sitting with kenny lewakowski outside of the infamous tippitinas jazz club in new orleans

"Welcome guys!" the manager greets us as we walk in. "Welcome to Tipps," he says again. "C'mon, I want to show you around, Derek, and introduce you to a few people."

I bounced around that place like a little boy with a free pass to check every single toy out. I looked in every corner, I touched every poster of prior stars playing there, and I simply was in complete joy mode as we made our way around the venue.

"Here is your dressing room, Derek."

"Really? This big room just for me?"

"Oh, no, Stanley will be in here with you, of course."

"You mean I get to actually hang out with Stanley?" I still couldn't believe what was transpiring. We walked back down the rear entrance to the stage, and there it was: instruments, lights, the whole shebang!

"Here is where you will set up, Derek."

"Excellent!"

I noticed a black baby grand piano covered with a blanket towards the back of the stage. "Kenny, why did we have to rent a piano?"

"I was told that's how it worked here," Kenny responded.

"What do you mean that's how it works, we just spent 200 bucks on a digital piano when I could be playing that thing?" I've always been a vocal guy, so I asked. "Hey, Mr. General Manager, why can't I use that big baby grand?"

"Mr. Jordan will be using that one, Derek."

"Oh, I see."

I was a bit bummed out that it took money I didn't have to find a piano to use for forty minutes. Paul ended up paying for the piano rental if I recall, as I was pretty much flat broke. But hey, I'm on the same stage as Stanley. I felt lucky indeed.

After finishing my sound check, Stanley quietly jumped on stage. He didn't have a manager, or anyone with him, just Stanley and a guitar strapped over his shoulder.

"I'm Derek, what a pleasure to meet you, Mr. Jordan."

"Hi, Derek," he said in a very soft and humble voice. I didn't want to seem like some freaky fan, so I made it rather quick not to waste much of his time with small talk.

I sat down on the right side of the stage while Stanley began sound check. "Kenny, I whispered. You really want me to go on stage before this guy? Listen to him play. I'm far from this level of talent, Ken."

"Don't be nervous, Derek, you both display your musical work in different shapes," he assured me.

"Oh, god, I'm not sure I can do this, Kenny."

"You will be fine. C'mon, let's go grab your clothes and relax in the dressing room.

with stanley jordan at tippitinas jazz club for sound check

I noticed all the fun little trinkets, photos, and the left-behind energy in this room that many gifted musicians had sat exactly where I was sitting.

"Hey, Derek, you sounded really great out there."

I looked over to see Stanley with a boatload of food in his arms, I believe all vegetarian items, still not sure to this day, my nerves were making me weird by this point. "Thank you, Stanley, that's super cool thing of you to say," I replied, although I don't think my sound check sounded that great, and Stanley was probably just giving me a little needed confidence push.

"Have some," he said as he pointed at all the food.

"Thank you, but I ordered a bunch of Mexican food." We sat and exchanged a few stories while eating. Stanley is a very soft-spoken man with a super warm energy to his presence. You could just feel his special energy. I picked away at my dinner as I emotionally prepared to get ready for my forty minutes on stage.

"Twenty minutes!" a voice shouted up to the room. Kenny came bouncing in, as he was down on the stage making sure everything was ready for me.

"Good luck, Derek!" said Stanley as I got up. He reached for my hand. I reached out feeling like I was about to be blessed by this famous musician before going on stage. It was so surreal that I can barely even remember my performance.

My entrance video and music started. "Three minutes, Derek," Kenny was now in supercharged mode, which gave me yet more confidence. I walked down the stairway that led me to the stage entrance. I closed my eyes, and suddenly the clapping and screaming welcome of people in the audience simply took me to a place I had never been. It was perfect. "It's all you, Derek," Kenny says with a huge smile on his face. He hugged me for a quick moment, and just like that, I walked out on stage glowing as if someone had stuck twenty-five glow sticks up my rear end.

Today, as I look back at this special experience, I'm not so sure if I could have walked out on that stage before Stanley Jordan without that simple handshake he offered me, or the hug Kenny gave me, or the encouragement from Paul. It was one of those moments that I am so blessed to have experienced, that I'm not sure if any live performance I do in the future could ever compare.

Stanley was so cordial, so composed, and simply brilliant to watch perform. I think it gave me confidence and a true sense of knowing I can do this. I will forever hold this as one of the very best musical experiences of my life. Thank you Tippitina's for the wonderful opportunity, and even more than that, thank you Stanley Jordan for reaching out to literally hold my hand for a moment before I entered that stage. How lucky am I to be able to say that one of my musical heroes actually pushed me out on that stage! And to Kenny and Paul for making this such a fantastic beginning to what would become my passion to express myself musically in a way I didn't even know possible!

One last note on this trip to New Orleans: We got back to Paul's house after the gig around 3:30 am.

"Kenny, make sure you set your alarm, we have to be at the airport in two hours."

"Got it set already, Derek!" came Ken's voice from the other bedroom. "Goodnight guys."

"Derek, Derek, get up, man!"

"What the hell, Kenny?"

"Its 7:00 am!"

"What?"

"We are late!" Kenny screams as he frantically runs around naked trying to find his clothes.

We couldn't afford to pay for another flight. "Ken, you better...."

"Hold on, Derek, I am on the phone with the airline."

"Why, Ken, our plane left thirty minutes ago." I was pissed off, only due to not having any sleep, my adrenaline still pumping from playing, and really not even all the way awake.

"I'm firing you, Kenny, if I don't get home today."

"How can you fire me, you can't even afford to hire me!" Kenny hollers while covering the phone so the airline rep wouldn't hear us arguing.

"I'm serious, Ken, you better get me on that plane."

"Hurry up, Derek, get dressed now."

Paul walks in. "What's going on guys?"

"Kenny overslept and we missed our flight."

"Oh, shit, you better get going!" Paul says.

"You guys quit talking so I can hear the lady on the phone."

Now Ken's getting pissed off. I grabbed my bags and threw it in Paul's very fast Mercedes. "I'm going to kill you, Kenny."

"Quiet, Derek, I'm almost done on the phone."

"Done!" he says.

"What do you mean done, Ken?"

"We have ninety minutes to get on the next plane."

"Go, go, go, go!" I said, pushing him out the door. Paul casually sat in the car waiting on us. That's what I love about Paul, always consistent with his demeanor.

golfing with paul in hollywood

"Get out and run, guys!" Paul pointing towards the airport entrance.

"Love ya, Paul!"

"Love ya, Derek."

"I hate you for this, Kenny."

"I love you too, Derek."

"You're an asshole Ken."

"Hey, you're getting home, aren't you?"

We made it home that day after all the confusion!

"Kenny?"

"Ya, Derek?"

"I love ya brother, let's go fishing."

TEN
All Work, No Play

Piecing together what I had learned from my experience working with Chemex Western in California, I put what little money I could come up with into a partnership with my longtime friend Darren, which would become Midwest Chemex.

My partner in the venture, an old school buddy, was unfamiliar with this type of work, although Darren was a hardworking guy and very smart. I knew I needed all the help I could get, and there was no way I could qualify for a business loan at that time. I called my Dad for a much needed push with financial assistance to make this work. My father always has a clever response when being asked for help.

"Derek, if you want this to work bad enough, you will go out and buy as many pencils as you can afford, sell them on the street corner for twice what you purchased them for, and in no time you will have some money to work with."

These clever comments would frustrate me as a young businessman, and of course stick with me through the years. Dad never did assist me financially with that venture, or any future ventures for that matter. It was always, "Do it on your own, Derek." He just like to word it a bit differently I suppose.

Darren was able to take a ten thousand dollar loan from the local bank. It was just enough for us to purchase a truck and equipment needed to barely get things rolling. The first year would be beyond challenging to the both of us, as a total of 12,000 dollars made for the year would not cut it, and we were beginning to struggle getting along simply due to the financial stress of our commitment.

I began working more and more hours, and slowly taking over most all aspects of running a new business.

"I can't afford this too much longer," Darren assured me.

"I know," I responded, "what am I supposed to do with 6,000 dollars for a whole year of work." I made it clear that the struggles were getting to me as well.

"You're going to have to buy me out," Darren quietly said.

"How am I going to do that? We made 12,000 between us, and winter is here."

"The mobile truck washing business was something I had obviously never attempted, as it was always sunny in California! I am going to focus on painting signs for the race track, and you can take over the business, pay me the 10,000-dollar loan back, and I'm sure it will work out for you, Derek."

The next few months of winter would prove to be too harsh. I made every attempt to work out in the coldest of days, in hopes to somehow come up with the money to pay Darren off.

After winter, Darren called me to make me aware that he had hired an attorney to settle matters. This hurt my heart, as I knew he was deserving of his investment back, but I was also pissed off that he walked out and left me holding all responsibilities of this debt we acquired. I was now stimulated by both frustration and a need to pay back a debt so I can move on and make a serious and valid attempt at building this company into something that would feed my family.

We ended up meeting at Darren's lawyer's office for a sit down, and their attempt to intimidate me as we shuffled through paperwork thrown out in front of me.

"Is your lawyer coming, Mr. Amato?"

"Pardon me?"

"I'm assuming your lawyer will be speaking on your behalf."

"Actually, it's just me today, Sir." I propped up in my chair, almost like boys in their teens puffing out their chests before a fistfight.

He began to pick at me, throwing rude comments around, as if I was going to budge from hearing legal jargon I was unfamiliar with.

"Did you want to sign here, Derek, and simply settle this out of court?"

"Well, I suppose I should." Darren was awarded the 10,000 to be paid back.

Regardless of the struggles, Darren and I would keep a distant friendship and respect for one another, and I still think highly of him today.

"I am going out to find some work!" I shouted to Donna as I made way out to my pickup truck. I knew I had to find work to fill in those cold Midwestern winter months, or this business was simply going to fail, and fail quickly.

I drove by the Kenworth dealership located in Sioux Falls, way out on the north side of town. Most trucking companies were out in this commercial area. Cold calling made me nervous, but I would somehow encourage myself to put my salesman shoes on and just bite the bullet. "Go in," I would persuade myself sitting in the parking lot of several trucking companies, "just go in." It would take a few of my self-coaxing words to get the ball rolling. People in the trucking business are fairly direct, which seemed to fit with my personality.

"Who do I talk to about cleaning your trucks?"

The secretary at Kenworth pointed to the office directly behind her. "Right there."

"Can I just go in?"

"You can ask him if he's busy."

I knocked, leaning around the door frame to peek in. "Excuse me, do you have a second?"

"Of course. Come in."

I pleaded my case for needing work, explaining that I had this amazing business of cleaning trucks. He listened patiently, looking back and forth from the papers on his desk back to me.

"Why don't you go over to that office over there across the way, and speak with Denton? That's his area."

"That works," I nodded. "What was your name, Sir?"

"Bill," as he reached out with this alarmingly huge hand.

"Nice to meet you, Bill," looking down to realize my hand was engulfed. Bill was a sizable guy. I knew he was an ex-jock just from his sturdy and confident presence.

"Are you Denton?"

"Yep."

"Can I speak with you for a minute?"

"Yep." Denton was a whole different color of character, and I was immediately intrigued by the guy.

"I'm Derek, nice to meet you." He shook my hand with a somewhat curious look on his face. I continued to pitch my business, and he finally stopped me.

"Let's go out back, Derek." Denton took me out back to what he called "The Boneyard."

"See that?"

"The blue truck?"

"Yep. Make it look new. I will give you 400 bucks," he firmly made me aware, "and not a dime more." I had to absolutely make the guy think I had much experience in the detailing industry, although it was my first job in regard to completely restoring a vehicle of that size. "And I need it done now."

"Like right now?"

"Yep."

"I can do that."

Fifteen days passed by rather quickly. Denton entered the building where I was working on the truck.

"You're not finished yet?"

"I'm close, Denton."

"You're not going to make any money if it's going to take you two weeks to get one of my trucks ready for sale."

I was thinking in the back of my head, *I really got screwed on this deal.* "I'm not sure if I can do trucks this size for 400 dollars, Denton."

"Derek, you told me you needed work. I don't care how you do it, just do it well, and get my stuff done in a timely fashion."

The next day as I was getting close to finally finishing, again walks in Denton.

"I think I will make some money on this old truck," he affirmed.

"That's good. I guess I did my job," cleaning the aluminum dust from my face after polishing the tanks.

"The tanks came out like shit," Denton said, pointing.

"I know, that's something I've never done."

"Here's your check, kid." Denton handed me a check for 650 dollars. This would become the beginning of a relationship that would not only build me into a fairly aggressive young business guy, but a friendship that would remain so very special to me.

I went on with the help from Denton to build my business into a thriving fairly decent moneymaking machine. I would spend countless hours at the shop trying to build this business into an empire—or at least a small one. I would employ more than seventy-five people during the next few years, and open locations in Sioux City, Iowa, and Denver, Colorado. Many stories would follow. Many lunches with Denton that would continue to escalate my business tactics, and of course, many ass chewings. Denton would challenge me nonstop to be the best in the business that I could.

After sending me out to learn how to polish aluminum truck gas tanks, several months later, it would become my primary source of income. Polishing truck tanks is physically demanding, not to mention the particles produced in the air by high-speed grinding wheels with potent compounds to breathe. It was one of the most physically challenging items to learn, but I would soon master the art of polishing, and the money was paving the way to success, or at least paying the bills.

My relationship with Denton and Bill at Kenworth would grow over the years, and I have always looked back at that opportunity they both gave me as one of the greatest gifts I have been given by anyone. I truly loved Denton as a friend, mentor, and very much a father figure.

Not long ago, I received an e-mail from Denton's oldest son, Chad. "We lost my father, Derek, I wanted to let you know right away."

I looked back at the many memories with Denton, reminding myself how lucky I was to love such a special man. During my last visit home, I was able to have lunch with him. It was on my bucket list to tell this man to his face just how important he was in my life. After telling Denton this, he looked at me and said, "You're a hardworking kid." That was my very last conversation with a man that I will miss dearly.

my mentor Denton Haber "heavy D"

By this time, Sydney and Morgan had joined our growing young family. It was a wonderful time in my life when the girls came into our world. It gave me even more motivation to build this so-called empire.

My resume was about to make many changes during the next several years, and after some financial struggles and the stress of working way too much, the physical labor tearing my body up, Donna announced we would be moving to Northern Colorado.

"Why Greeley?" I asked her.

"It's where my parents decided to move to, Derek. My dad is moving his business there, and my mother is also opening her business there." Although a shocking and quick announcement, I was actually eager to try something new.

"Isn't Greeley a big baseball community?"

"I'm not sure," she responded, as we began the packing process all over again.

I started looking into the baseball programs in this small northern Colorado community. Sure enough, baseball is the sport of choice, and heavily supported by the community. *This will work out perfect*, I thought to myself. *I will be able to coach Alex through the system there*, which in fact would come to life, just shortly after our arrival.

"What's that smell!" I blurted out, making a yuck face.

"That's the Monfort thing," Donna said.

"What's a Monfort thing? It smells like shit."

"It is shit," Donna replied, laughing. "It's the Monfort family, they own the meat plant and the huge lot of cows out that way," pointing just east of where we moved into. "My mom cuts her hair."

"Whose hair?"

"Mr. Monfort's wife."

"Oh, I see."

My resume would continue to take some turns in and out of a few jobs that I just couldn't fit into. Finally landing a sales job for Toyota, I would meet Gerry, Jeff, and Steve, my first official friends, and my Colorado experience was now underway. I loved it here—well, not necessarily Greeley, but it was close enough to the mountains, the streams, sports, and Denver is just an hour drive up the road.

with jeff and gerry gomez for the brain injury charity

Continuing my efforts to make Alex into the best baseball player on the planet, I was thrilled to learn of his abilities as a left-handed pitcher. This was fantastic, as I knew I could get him off to a great start, and at that time, our many hours spent together on the dirt would become our haven together. From early on, Alex was a challenging personality as an athlete. Stubborn doesn't come close to describing this kid on the field. There is a fine line not to be crossed when it's a father-son coaching situation.

I pushed Alex harder than most children, simply because there was a noticeable difference of athleticism he portrayed early on. I was cautious not to overstep my boundaries of pushing too hard, and, at times, it seemed he would actually push me beyond my limits. Actually, I pushed all the children during my coaching years. I always believed in the design of coaching kids to be better people, which would enhance their natural abilities as a player. I taught these children to build a friendship amongst themselves that no other team had, and it worked. My rewards came in so many different shapes from coaching. The joy of watching these kids build a family of players that was so close is exactly what made their winning spirit a force of intensity on the playing field. I recall a very warm afternoon with the baseball team at the park for practice. Alex and I had a disagreement about something, obviously not too important, as I don't recall what the topic was being argued about.

Alex decided to simply not give in to my request, and, somehow, I ended up instructing him to go run a few laps and think about it. Well, the few laps turned into several, and I screamed to him, "Come here, son, let's talk about it!" His response was simple. He would not even look at me, and he continued running laps for another forty-five minutes, at which time I had come to the conclusion that he would make an amazing cross country runner for any track team. He didn't like running, but on this occasion, I think he loved running and would run as long as it took to win this argument with me. I gave in. He stopped running, and still insisted on ignoring my attempts to apologize for the misunderstanding, and I told him, "You're one of those special athletes, Alex, and I love you."

Coaching Alex stands at the top of my list of most special life experiences. It gave us much time to learn one another, challenge one another, and simply be boys together. I didn't live my baseball fantasies though my son, and I truly know I crafted one amazing baseball player. He allowed me to share my passion for the game through his talent, patience for a driving coach, and love for his father. This was a pure experience with the two of us, and we carry the memories with us both everyday to this very moment.

I groomed not only very talented young baseball players, but even more so, I was a part of stimulating positive growth amongst these kids, my son included. I often get random reminders, as every great once in a while I open up my e-mail box to find a "Thank you coach" from one of the boys. This would be the truest meaning of residual income, although in the shape of a simple, gracious e-mail.

My life would become most challenging in Greeley, Colorado, as Donna and I preparing to divorce would strain each of us to limits beyond hurt. I went on my way in 1997, after a long and frustrating last four years of marriage. By this time, Donna's physical and emotional outbursts were tearing me down, not to mention putting our children in a position that would hurt them for many years to follow.

alex, sydney, and morgan growing up

The move to Greeley would put me into a tailspin that would take me fifteen years to recover from, financially and emotionally. The damage had been done. Much of it, I believe, was fueled by a family used to having alcohol in their everyday lives. The consistent behaviors that both Donna and her parents would surround us with would become a battle in our everyday living. Drama, alcohol, drama, and more alcohol … I've always believed firmly that alcohol will demolish a family, destroy lives, and amplify even the smallest of battles … hence, the reason I have never been into drinking.

"I'm calling the cops!" Donna screamed out at me while she was smashing me in the face with a large hairbrush. My eye was now bleeding as I made every attempt to just hold her down to discontinue her beating on me. Striking a woman has never been something I have done, but at this moment, I was near breaking, plus, my physical well being was actually being threatened by a female. I never did end up lashing out or striking her during that struggle, or any confrontation for that matter.

Getting her to the floor was my only option to try and keep her confined, as I was trying to dial the police. I made it out the door finally after receiving several kicks to my crotch and pelvic area, as she slammed the door to ensure I was outside. The glass window in the door made it easy to verbally exchange a few cuss words between us, and suddenly, out of nowhere, I feel glass explode in my face, and I knew I hadn't headbutted the window. She had punched through the door's glass window in attempts to punch me in the face. I was bleeding from the tiny cuts. The cops finally pulled in. No one was even given a ticket for domestic violence, rather instructed to go about our own ways.

Of course, this altercation stimulated a heated exchange between Donna's father and me, and before I knew it, he was banging on my door threatening to kick my ass. I answered, we argued for a few minutes, and I made myself very clear I would never allow his daughter to physically hurt me and my children again. There would come more physical threats from Donna, with many scratch marks, cuts, bruises, and scars left on my body from being banged on. I was now running out of patience with not only physical abuse, but the fact of knowing my children were being exposed to such harm; a family of alcoholics was literally destroying my family, children and all.

Finding a stable position and job that would challenge me would be trying during this transition in my life. If not being stimulated and challenged in the fiercest of ways, I would grow tired of a job. I wasn't designed to sit back with a company for five or ten years without constant challenge—just not possible for my mindset.

I knew if I stayed as busy as I could that I would not put myself anywhere near these individuals, and I did just that. Teaching karate, a stint with a gas and oil company, a Schwan's truck driver, a public relations director, a sales manager—you name it, I dabbled in many, making my resume to date pretty damn interesting to say the least.

The aftereffects of my choices to stay busy wouldn't hit me until later in my life. I know that my desire to work so often would affect my children in a way that I had no idea, as many stories can be told to young children by one parent when the other is out chasing a career path. Regardless, I would pay for my lack of making knowledgeable and solid choices in regard to my career path and stability.

There seems to be a price tag on all we do through this life journey. Working too much affects the presence of a father figure, traveling in search of a better job creates the same, but even more than that, it was my way out of abuse, and I knew there would come a time when my children would be at ages of understanding some of these struggles and decisions I had made prior. It has always been a challenge to speak on these topics, as they are still painful items that simply take time to heal. I am a very lucky father, as my relationship with each of my three children is something beyond special, and I truly have a love affair with each of them. My ex-wife simply never bonded with them as babies; it was evident from day one as they each entered this world. It truly hurt my soul, as I always wanted to see

Donna enjoy that process each and every mother deserves—actually, I'm not so sure every mother deserves it. I think it is more of "Every parent is allowed the opportunity to make such a special connection" experience, rather deserving—deserving sounds free to me. Experiences such as bonding with a child are a gift and should be earned in my humble opinion.

My career path was starting to look up as I joined a nonprofit organization specializing in the education of youth safety welfare. This was right up my alley, as I was a karate kid, and I could certainly talk circles around many now that I had been properly trained in business negotiations by the great Heavy D (Denton). This was Eric's given nickname to Denton—it just stuck.

I started as an instructor—and I ended up becoming the director of public relations for this firm—and yet I met another motivating individual who would inspire me: Ron! This was a fairly short experience, as we simply had different views about how to raise money for manageable youth safety programs throughout North America. It was a fantastic experience, as I would often find myself at meetings surround by sixty-five-year-old board members, making me the youngest voice at the table, and I loved that position and challenge.

We made a difference as I look back, instructing literally thousands of children throughout the country, certainly one of my most prized accomplishments to date.

That quick vacation Mike and I would take to Montreal would be a forever changing factor in my next attempt at self-employment. Being raised in the karate studio since the day I can remember has much to do with my competitive spirit—yes, even to this very moment as I write this book. I just didn't realize how much those early karate days with Dad would influence my professional path.

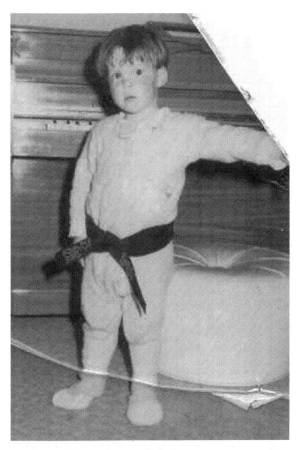

i was born with a karate belt on

I had grown up with a firm martial arts childhood, and it carried on as a young adult as I became intensely interested in jujitsu. Somewhat straying away from my traditional studies of kung fu san soo, it was fascinating to me, this art of fighting on the ground. Those many years my father studied with the great Jimmy Woo would be transferred to my always growing interest in the arts.

"Can you leave next week?" I screamed across the shop to Michael. Of course, even he had been a given nickname by Eric, and so it went we always refer to Michael as "Slim." I'm serious, Eric had a nickname

117

for every single person who worked for me, and extended out with our common friends.

"Where do you want to go, Amato?"

"Rick Roufus is fighting in the kickboxing championships against Theriault, the Canadian guy."

"Who?"

"C'mon, it will be fun! Plus, I need a vacation badly."

Donna and I had separated at that time. I had recently moved into an old trailer out on the west side of town.

"I will pay for the entire trip," I assured Slim, as I continued to tell him of the combatants who would be competing. I just couldn't get enough; boxing, karate, any shape of competition made me jump at the chance to attend.

"Where in Canada?" Slim was just starting to polish a tank.

"Montreal!" I answered loudly in my fighting fan voice. Six days later, we were on a plane to Montreal, and I had managed to get excellent seats. I also made arrangements to attend the afterfight party.

Montreal seemed to be an always turned on city, as 3:00 am downtown was as bright as if the sun never went down, lights everywhere. I made reservations and requested the top floor. For some reason, I have always loved staying as high up as I could get when in a hotel. I'm not fond of heights, but it seemed grander to me for one reason or another. I wanted to meet all the fighters and dragged Slim around like some overly excited little kid begging to show his parents a new toy. Slim obliged, as he also was fascinated with the whole experience.

The fights were just as good as I hoped they would be, and squirreling through the crowd afterwards was also part of the fun, as getting to the fighters for a quick hello was one of my favorite things to do—still is.

"Let's go eat something before we go to the party," Slim suggested, as we had sipped on a few beers during the fights, certainly not in excess, but enough to leave us feeling hungry after the show. We walked around after taking a taxi downtown, looking up at the tall building. I recall these small store front windows selling sex, like the old days of a pretty woman standing in a window for sale, yes, a real live prostitute. I wasn't accustomed to seeing anything of the sort, and I admit, it caught me off guard a bit.

We grabbed a bite to eat at a diner that was buzzing with people. "Let's get going, the party has started, Derek." I finished my burger and fries and off we went.

"Where is your pass I gave you, Slim?"

"What pass?"

"I put it in with your airline ticket."

"No you didn't." He was correct, no I didn't. We scrambled back to the hotel, and sure enough, passes were in my bag, right where I put them. Finally down to the bottom floor of the hotel, we flagged another taxi.

"Take us to the big party over at the...."

"What's the name of the place" Slim asked me.

"It's on the ticket," I told him, as I couldn't remember where it was taking place.

"Here you are...."

"How much do we owe you?"

"Forty-five dollars."

I jumped out in a hurried fashion, aware that a few celebrity martial artists would be present. We mingled with everyone we could. It was a surprisingly tame crowd, and the party was nicely put together.

"There he is Slim!"

"Who?"

"You know, remember the movie *Kickboxer* with Van Damme?"

"Ya, I don't see Van Damme, though, Derek."

"No, the other guy, dumb ass," I said, almost rudely pointing so Slim could visually connect. "It's Dennis Alexio. He is the world heavyweight champion, I think. Let's go say hello," I chanted.

Dennis was a really super humble man to chat with, even with a little shiner around his eye; he had taken a pretty good shot during his fight, but ended up with a win, a serious win. This guy is a beast of a fighter.

"There he is!" I said again to Slim. It was getting exciting now, with a buzz and energy to the room of guests that you could just feel. I loved it.

"Who?"

"Don the Dragon, can you believe it?" I don't think I waited for Slim to follow me this time, and I made a mad dash to meet one of my childhood heroes face-to-face. I noticed how big his hands were when I reached out to shake. Once again, a super soft-spoken athlete, but he was a little more articulate than most; well, go figure, he was an actor in Hollywood making karate movies. It was absolutely a highlight of my trip to Montreal. 2:30-ish came quickly. I didn't want the party to end, I was on a mission to meet everyone.

"Let's go folks," a voice over a speaker system announced, "time to go!"

We took a few more photos, grabbed a bottle of water off the bar that was put out for guests, and headed out to flag down yet another taxi ride. It was quickly becoming a fairly expensive trip, but I had the mentality at that time that I was going to have fun, period. Slim was still all pumped up from both fights and party, but it was getting late, now 3:00 am.

"I'm hungry," Slim announced.

"Again?"

"Drop us off right here, Sir." The taxi cab immediately pulled over. We walked another couple hundred yards in search of a late night diner, and, to no one's surprise, many places were open and available to walk into at that time of the day and order whatever you wanted. Again, I noticed how bright it was in the middle of the night there; seemed weird, yet interesting how a city just stays up all night.

This was the beginning of my professional experience working in the martial arts industry, dating back from 1993 through 2002. I produced sixty-five professional fights, managed a fairly significant group of fighters, and even attempted commentating for a pay per view in Canada, which didn't exactly work out as well as I had planned, but this would also be my introduction to another long-lasting and very special friendship with Mark and the maximum fighting championships.

Slim and I returned home to Sioux Falls with memories we would share stories of for many years to come, and he would remain one of my closest confidants.

By this time, I was working way too many hours, traveling way too much for any healthy lifestyle, and my working efforts would certainly impact my children's fears of not having Dad around enough. I've seemingly had this desire to chase a dream regardless of the pain and suffering some of my ventures would bring upon my life and family.

Looking back, I still carry guilt in my heart for missing moments with my children, but in my heart, I knew I would never settle, or even come close to finding or even providing happiness to others when I wasn't happy in my own skin.

I do in fact miss working in the martial arts. It's a very special group of athletes, and has a camaraderie of a wonderful circle of people to be involved with. In retrospect, I was simply ahead of my time, as shortly after I went broke from producing the biggest show card of my career, the *Ultimate Fighter* would shock the airwaves, bringing the mixed martial arts to another level in the public view. Timing wasn't right, and I simply didn't have the funding to produce a television situation.

My memories are many in this most passionate love affair I have with the martial arts, but I don't think I will be jumping into the ring any time soon. It's a young man's game nowadays, and I'm content sitting back knowing I had a most amazing experience, and the friends I made will last forever.

My trip to see Mark in Edmonton would stick with me forever. Jake and I entered the event as business partners, friends, and I his manager ... and we weren't leaving without the championship belt. Yes, Jake took home the belt, and this was my first and only time being booed by a bunch of angry Canadian fans that my guy just knocked out!

Mark still inspires me with his zest and savvy business mind, always going 100 mph working in the martial arts industry, and I have become quite fond of Canada.

I have been back to Canada many times since my work in the martial arts, and I've come to enjoy the people and a quality of life that is very appealing to me.

Eh!

with dennis hallman and mark pavelich for the maximum fighting championships in Canada, my guy won!

Moments

singing with prodigious savant Tony DeBlois at the Haiti Charity

hanging out with the kids at the Boys and Girls Club, Sioux Falls, SD.

fun times with Rob Schneider in Denver, CO.

with Mark Cuban during The Jeff Probst Show in Los Angeles

the "real" breakfast club!

dialing Santa for my brother

Dino the 60's in California

some friends with me for The Jeff Probst Show taping in Los Angeles.

trying my best to persuade Jeff Probst to put me on Survivor!

in the backyard with the kids

with Bobby Marlow in the ring with all the girls, my kids and cousins!

the infamous Gary Lennox at Dog House Music Studios

with Gerry for the brain injury charity

with Kathy Goss (my favorite teacher) at Whittier Jr. High School, Sioux Falls, SD.

i met Greg(homeless) while doing a photo shoot out in the mountains.

with Jake Hattan, R.J Cline, and my brother Dino, during a Millennium Sport Fighting mixed martial arts event.

with Dusdi Fissette for rehearsals at the 2013 Grammys in Los Angeles

clowning around with Brendon Villegas from Big Brother

a moment with Nora Jones at the 2013 Grammy Awards

my one and only niece, Addisyn!

with Simon Hammond in Canada for photo shoot

standing on the ledge 15 stories from the ground with Anastacia Wilhite for a photo shoot in Hollywood.

i am number 2. we miss you #4 Todd Putzier!

walking the last section with Nate Jorgenson for the Shared Journeys Brain Injury Charity event in Colorado.

my brother and I started driving at
an early age

im not sure why mom had me in a suit

my brother and I with my
grandparents, Olga and Joe

the only photo of my parents,
Pete and Shelley

stopping in at the local dairy queen, Greeley, CO

my favorite photographer to work with, Sean Hartgrove

the wonderful Dr. Tom and my daughter Morgan. He is one special man!

with Jack Black at the Lifetime Achievement Awards and 2013 Grammy Awards.

my brother and I begging for a ride in the cop car with grandpa Joe.

with Josh and Dan at Tony's in Fort Collins, CO.

with Teri and Tim Katzenberger in Sioux Falls, SD.

after The Today Show in New York, hanging with the kids!

photo shoot with Rose Pettibone, 2 weeks after my accident.

with the Shared Journeys Brain Injury organization in Fort Collins, CO.

always loved the hair styles
mom would come up with

meeting everyone outside after The
Today Show with Matt Lauer

with Simon Hammond in
Canada for photo shoot

raising money with team gourmet for
Michelles Place and breast cancer

floating down the Arkansas River with Lalena Kotsek for photo shoot in Salida, CO.

hanging out with Ann Curry and Matt Lauer after my interview on The Today Show

with my son Alex after filming with The Today Show at Dog House Music Studios

digging for gold in the Rocky Mountains with Steve "Walleye Guy" Burgess

with my father and brother Dino for the Millennium Sport Fighting event at the Filmore Auditorium in Denver, CO.

hanging out with my grandson Dallas, my best friend!

April and I on set filming with The Discovery Science Channel.

with my children after filming The Today Show pre interview at Dog House Music Studios in Colorado.

with my lifelong friend Tom Ecker at The Jeff Probst Show

my brother and I with Addisyn

talking weather with Al Roker

with Mark and Christy Shipley, my handlers for the Reality Rally Charity event. I love these two people!

a whole bunch of reality tv stars for the Reality Rally Charity for Michelles Place.

a good luck kiss from my mother before my interview with Matt Lauer

ELEVEN
Someone To Lean On

Most of the time, it makes me feel somewhat euphoric when playing the piano, although, when not playing, there are many moments of feeling overstimulated and mentally exhausted from a musically always turned on brain. Coping would be a struggle during these last six years, always trying to find a way to slow my mind down. I have found it important to continue on my quest of "taming the composition." Hiking, walking, fly fishing …I'm getting there. Fly fishing seems to allow my brain a moment to rest—not completely, but so far the best tool I've found to assist me in finding balance.

with my brother dino fishing the fryin pan river in Basalt, Colorado.

It's become a part of my life now, allowing me to share this experience with many. From day one of my discovery, I knew it would be so important for me to display myself in a way that would allow my gift to open up a treasure chest of possibilities and ideas to my children, not to mention the world looking in. But how do they benefit from all of this? I continually found myself asking. "It's a gift," Jason would remind me daily, "it's supposed to be shared."

There has been a caution in this process of who I let in close enough to truly understand this journey my brain is on. In the beginning, I found comfort in reaching out to Dr. Darold Treffert, as his input and guidance displayed sincere care with unquestionable compassion. I would meet many people throughout the last seven years, not just medical practitioners, but everyone, from film producers to journalists, seemingly pulling at me from all directions, making this whole process a bit overwhelming, which naturally would be difficult for anyone to process.

There is a natural progression to all of this, or should I say, I have chosen the other path, so to speak. I knew there would come a time when I would have to decide how to "share my gift" and make this new musical discovery a viable situation to be able to actually call it a career. This area of my concern would rely heavily on who I would choose, or, I should say, "who I would trust" on my team.

The list of individuals seemingly decreased over the last few years, as it really is true what they say in show business, "Your immediate circle of friends WILL become few," although I have never really looked at it like that, as I have preferred to constantly remind myself of my father's most famous six words to me since childhood, "Count on nothing but your fingers, Derek."

"You simply can't do everything by yourself," Jason would constantly remind me. "There are several different people you are going to have to let in sooner or later, Derek."

"I realize that, but it's very challenging when everyone seems to be more interested in making money off my life story rather wanting to personally become a part of this team, Jason."

"Here is a list, Derek, go through it when you have a moment."

"What kind of list?"

"Like I said, people that you are going to need assistance from. Your life is becoming very busy, Derek. You are doing speaking engagements, live musical performances, public appearances, and your involvement with charitable organizations is taking a great amount of your time, and I haven't even mentioned the many hours you spend in the studio composing, or as you put it, 'decompressing.'"

"This list is a bunch of people, Jason. How do we bring them in when I am barely making enough money to support myself?"

"I'm working on it, Derek, and I think it's very important we start at the top of the list. A lawyer, a publicist, a manager…."

"I don't see 'assistant' listed on here anywhere?"

"That would be a bonus position, Derek, you probably won't get an assistant for a while."

"But that's the one person I need the most right now. I'm overloaded with daily work, and that is the frustrating part, as I can't make my way to the studio often enough to let all this music in my head escape."

"I realize that, but the next few months will be very busy, and we will have to find a release for you, maybe bring your fly rod with you when traveling."

As several months pass by, I had still not been able to put together this "dream team" of needed people to assist in my daily work, although we have had meetings with all of the listed important people on Jason's list.

"Did you review the stuff I sent you, Derek?"

"I did, and I sat down and checked off all of the individuals we talked to."

"What do you mean checked them off?"

"I checked off the ones that didn't seem to fit?"

"You mean you checked off all of them that you refuse to trust?"

"Kind of. I didn't connect with any of them, Jason. I'm building a family, bro. I've always believed the key to one's success lies upon how your team players are treated, and I treat everyone that works with and for me 'as family,' you know this, Jason. It takes the right chemistry to build an empire, you know?"

"I agree," Jason said, shaking his head as if I were being difficult.

"How many times have I brought friends into this journey and allowed them to use their talent to contribute to this, Jason?"

"I know, Derek, but it takes a special individual to tolerate the bumps and bruises of this industry."

"I know. It really is amazing to watch the process, Jason."

"What do you mean, Derek?"

"I can't just sit here and expect my friends to work with and for me for free, and on the other hand, when someone does tolerate the struggle standing next to me without swaying, it truly shows that we are sharing a dream together, like I said earlier, as a team."

"That's in a perfect world, Derek, but I do agree, it's a challenging process finding the right personalities to bring in to assist."

jason and I chatting with chris rock after the today show interview.

The kids have accepted this transition in my life in a very humble and supportive way. Sydney and Morgan never wanted to take me to show and tell, they didn't walk around the school halls screaming "My dad's a savant!" and, quite honestly, the topic is seldom brought up. I think we all look at it as a gift; of course, all of us with a different explanation and definition of the word "miracle." Things are a bit different now since being on television, as the kids are approached by their peers with inquisitive questions, comments, and ooohs and aaaahs. I think now as young adults, all of this makes them smile when one of their friends asks them in regard, as just the other day, I caught Sydney shining as she gave her coworker a signed magazine interview I had recently finished. I could see it a mile away, she had the "That's my dad" look stamped on her forehead.

I've always insisted my children enjoy this journey with me. Sydney and Morgan are usually by my side for events, appearances, interviews, etc.... They are my helpers, not to mention my support, as I get so excited when out and about, continually keeping me close, knowing I could collapse from overstimulation at any given time, or simply just feeling sick from the excitement. The girls know how to handle me, I guess, they understand precisely how to calm me before I nervously walk on stage, and they keep me feeling safe, loved, and understood. My son Alex, on the other hand, usually stays fairly quiet in the background looking in, although I see the excitement in his eyes watching his father share life with many. Alex has a firm outlook as to my newfound career. "Make it a job that supports your family," period. Although he in fact supports my creative business ideas most all the time, he just looks at it all very simply, "My dad has a gift, my dad has three children, make it happen," or find a real job and get over it. Matter a fact, my daughters probably agree with that perspective just as much as he does, and quite honestly, how can I not agree?

There is a loneliness that comes to working in the entertainment industry. I'm not talking about the typical stresses of who to trust in Hollywood. It's the little things that become factors in your daily habits. Traveling becomes a way of life, a suitcase becomes your very small closet, and your own voice becomes your confidant. There is no wonder why very few people get to work at high levels in this business. It takes not only a rare bird, but these people are truly the best of the best, no different from playing professional sports, only a few make it and can deal with it.

from big, to small

During the last few years, I have become more aware of the needed tools to survive and make it in show business; not that I've made it by any means, although I have certainly been able to put a dent in the forward process of escalating my career in music and television by simply using tons of advice from many in the business. Often, I was told, "Trust no one," "You have no friends in Hollywood," and "They will eat you alive," you get my point. Most of these slogans are thrown about by frustrated actors and musicians who have struggled with careers in the entertainment business, and, yes, many of them far more talented than myself.

Imagine hearing that input more than needed, I mean, how hard is it for someone to say, "You're on your way to the top, kid," or "You're getting there." It's almost a preprogrammed message to everyone walking into Hollywood, no different from welcoming your coworker to hell. "Hey, you're going to love it here, care to join me while I burn?" I can think of better ways to inspire the aspiring musician or actor.

I will more than likely never be a huge rock star or television personality, this I understand. What I do know is that I simply want to be able to share my story in hopes of giving hope, faith, and even a simple smile to a stranger. My musical discovery has simply become a vehicle for me to expose the fantastic charity organizations I believe in, travel, and build a wealth of new friends who have joined me in my quest to give back. It really is that simple to me, always telling my children, "I am here to serve and love." I hope this infects them each with urgency in their purpose to give back and share life with many—it's working....

"Hey, Dad, will you ever get married again?" My relationship status has at times been in question through the last almost twenty years of life by my children. After my divorce, I really didn't go on some dating train ride. I did, in fact, start dating, although I am extremely consistent in this department. I would spend the next seventeen years with just a few relationships, each lasting two to four years. Once again, I found myself if not constantly challenged by a partner, indeed, I would grow bored, the relationship would come to a screeching stop, and I would take a year off to collect myself from my feeble attempt at building a truly successful situation with a partner.

Many of these recent experiences in my life have pushed me into discovering a different Derek. It's almost as if I have unlocked this curious part of my soul, and to even allow another person to actually get close to me, discover me, learn me, love me ... this has been a tough process to watch unfold, as going through this musical discovery process has literally changed my whole design. Even though my raw personality is very much charged by those I surround myself with in my daily life, I live a simple life, as I have grown numb to the struggles and challenges. Yes, I am responsible for inviting this new career in to my life, I own that, and I regret not one moment.

Not all experiences in this musical journey have been all rainbows and butterflies. It has challenged some closest to me, to a point where friendships have been lost, the many years put into the building of such friendships right out the window. Jealousy I'm sure has been a situation with a few. Either way, all of them have been hard to emotionally deal with and accept. Few have not swayed: Jason, Wayne, Rick, Steve, and of course, my mother and children.

It has never seemed fair to me how someone so close to me would struggle with jealousy, and or even a cynical outlook as to how I was sharing my life work, as my intent has always been to make it a true team journey. It makes sense to me to build a team of people I trust and can rely on. It takes many to make efforts possible on a bigger stage, and I have stayed consistent with the overall intent and concept of my goals, which is to give back, and everyone close to me understands this dream of mine. I even have a rule: Everyone who works for me must be active in a charitable organization—everyone!

As I was sitting at the park one afternoon pondering my life goals, it actually struck me: I found myself giving back more to charity than I actually earned towards financially taking care of my own responsibilities. I came to terms with understanding what it's like to live with nothing.

"If you are giving back more than you earn, Derek, it's apparent you belong in this position of giving," Jason assured me.

"I don't need much to survive, Jason. I realize that, Derek, but you have to have a home and a few other things to have your own comfort and stability."

"Are you sure I'm not just some nutty gypsy, Bro?" Jason was now laughing off my sarcasm.

I am fascinated with this area of life. Homelessness has become a monster I am adamant to taming. Why? Not just because I have been there, its more than that. I feel connected. I feel trusted when amongst them doing what I do best, sharing love and genuine care. Maybe I should just hire a team of homeless individuals to run the team, I mean c'mon, whats the difference between a well suited agent in Hollywood that you don't know? One wants money for a Mercedes payment, the other to simply eat. I choose to feed my team rather make their car payment. Don't get me wrong here, I want everyone to financially prosper from my life work and efforts, I just want them to be hungry with the same desire to give back.

on the streets in San Diego

On the flip side, you can't imagine the harsh exchanges that transpire between my brother and me. I am simply out of patience with attempting to explain my purpose, my passion, my gift, and I'm most certainly worn out from being told to "go get a real job."

It takes a very special individual to not only understand my current design, but to truly see into me deep enough to understand my purpose and tolerate the many glitches that come with an ordinary guy with a strange gift.

Leaning trees in this business are hard to come by!

TWELVE
Lemon Trees and Roses

As I clawed my way back, first taking a job as a mailman, I had handled just about everything fate had thrown my way. I just needed one more break.

After meeting Sean Fair, I was hired on with a telecommunications company. I excelled in my role and advanced quickly. I actually loved this job, and it would introduce me to Jason Drenner, whom I mention several times in this book.

I had no idea how lucrative the cell phone industry really was. It wasn't until a couple of weeks later that I was introduced to the owner of the company. I remember walking down the hallway of the corporate office located in sunny San Diego. Sean assured me I was going to love John. "He's a very aggressive guy. C'mon, Derek, let's see if he's in."

"Good afternoon," I was greeted by John as he sat behind his desk. He stood to shake my hand. Hello, Sir, I'm Derek."

After all I had been told about John, I had already somewhat shaped my own vision of who and what to expect. I was completely off. He was much shorter, and completely not the staunch, uptight typical business executive I was expecting. John had an explosive energy, one of those infectious auras. One of those guys who started selling cell phones out of the trunk of his car, grabbed a handful of his close friends who were all from big name colleges, and bam, just like that, a money-making machine giving many the opportunity to splurge and enjoy the finer things in life, like renting out the band "minni kiss" for our corporate party, or a yacht to celebrate and sing karaoke, or ... well, you get my point.

This job wasn't for the soft-hearted. The travel schedule was grueling, although there was something that always excited me when going into a new city. My title at this time of employment was national corporate trainer. I directed the management staff of the training division of the western United States, and would spend three weeks of each month flying city to city. Dallas would become a favorite of stops, although the challenge of dealing with their market director would certainly have a twisted start.

Walking into the office of the Dallas market made me feel like I was waiting for someone to snap their fingers, and, suddenly, I would be attacked by the leader warriors from out of nowhere.

The secretary walked me back. "Derek, this is Mr. Arradondo." I just knew that very moment, I mean, this guy was staring me dead in the eyes with that "You're in my house" look, and he was dressed to the nines, and, quite honestly, simply a beautiful man.

the only "boss" in Dallas, Gilberto Arredondo

Mr. Arradondo was precisely to the point as to how his market was ran, and I was most certain there was to be an eye poked out rather a hug during this meeting. We both seemed to nonchalantly proceed to making it closer to lunch without a full blown disagreement as to business ideas.

"What do you like to eat, Amato?"

"Pardon me?"

"Eat, it's lunch time."

"I'm good with whatever you want, Arredondo."

"Excellent, let's go."

Before leaving the office, there would be one last discrepancy between the two of us hardheaded leaders.

I leaned over in hopes of no one hearing. "Listen to me, Arredondo, we can either do this together as a team, or you and I can go out back and settle this whenever you're feeling up to it."

"Anytime," he responded most confidently. "Let's go, I'm hungry, Derek, and call me Gil."

Gilberto and I would continue our professional relationship, making fantastic changes to the Dallas market with successful results. I had found this most amazing man that not only challenged me, but actually intimidated me with his brilliance. Today, I am blessed to call Gilberto one of my dearest friends, mentors, and yes, he still challenges me—in a good way, of course.

Serendipity was apparent for the first time in decades, and I had met Renee on the dance floor of a club in Denver called Polyesters. Earlier that day, Chris had asked me to go out to Denver. It was an hour drive, and we weren't expecting it to be a late night, just a couple beers, some people watching, and ... there she was.

"Dude, look at that girl dancing with that guy over there."

"Where?"

"Right there," I replied as I reached over and turned his chin in the right direction. Chris was a very charismatic, charming, and good-looking guy, and always smiling with curiosity.

"The Mexican girl?"

"Ya."

"Is that her husband she's dancing with?"

"Oh, c'mon, there's no way, Chris, that has to be a courtesy dance."

"Can't you find a girl that's *not* dancing with a guy, Derek?"

"I'm going in; here, hold my beer."

I wasn't sure how to approach this situation, as I'm not really that good at walking up to a couple on a disco floor, and to make matters worse, the dude was really into the girl, or at least he sure looked absorbed.

"Excuse me," I said, tapping the guy on the shoulder the old-fashioned way, "do you mind if I dance with her for a song?"

He gave me the strangest look. "Um, ya, go ahead."

It worked; he actually didn't have a problem with me interrupting at all. I was relieved, as I was now so nervous I couldn't think of anything to say, so we danced and danced, and then finally introduced

Chris to her girl friend. I kind of felt guilty not paying attention to Chris, but I knew if I let her go, that dude would swoop back in, as I could feel him watching us the entire time.

"It's late, we have to go, Derek."

"Okay, give me two minutes, Chris."

"Would it be all right if I call you sometime? Actually, what is your name?"

"Renee."

"Great to meet you, Renee." As she leaned over to give me a hug, I thought, *What the heck, at least give it a shot.*

"Is there any chance you would take me home with you tonight?"

"Pardon me?"

"I was thinking I could go home with you tonight. I would sleep on the couch." Do all guys say that? Who sleeps on a couch when overwhelmed with such excitement?"

"Absolutely not," Renee responds as she reached in her purse.

I couldn't do or say anything after her response, but to only portray the face of a very sad puppy dog.

"Here, this is my number, call me sometime." Renee gave me a hug goodbye, and Chris and I drove home.

I couldn't wait anymore than the next day 10:00 am to call her.

with renee in sturgis, south Dakota (not my bike)

For the next four years, I worked around the clock regularly in an effort to try and make up for lost opportunities while basking in the glory of a committed relationship with a beautiful and caring woman.

But 100-hour work weeks eroded my personal life and, after four years, my relationship was on the rocks and my health in even worse condition.

There was no small talk. The doctor told me a growth on my colon had led to the almost 60-pound weight loss. Here I had thought all along that my weight loss was the outcome of my morning walks. It had become habit for me to take early morning walks while making my East Coast conference calls.

"You should consider making changes, before your health decides your future for you," said the doctor, employing a refreshingly frank bedside manner.

I had barely been able to admit it to myself, but I saw this coming—all of it. Throwing myself into my job with the same unrelenting focus I applied to baseball as a kid was always going to have a physical cost.

And suddenly, but not entirely unexpectedly, I was forced to shed more than weight: my relationship was over and my job eliminated.

I knew at that very moment I had to make an immediate adjustment. I was sick.

"Good morning," I said, trying to display my best, happy voice.

Alec responded curiously. "What's going on, Derek?"

"Can I come down for a while?"

"Of course, when you coming?" I can leave soon. I'm driving down, so I have to pack some stuff and change oil in the Mercedes."

"Fantastic…," Alec, always inviting, said, as I knew he knew something wasn't quite right.

Taking a break in the sun in Phoenix to get my health back at the invitation from Alec wasn't an indulgence, it was a necessity.

Alec was a most amazing host. After a few days of settling in, Alec comes home early from the office. Here, Derek, I got you a MacBook today."

"What?"

"A laptop, silly."

"You have to be kidding?"

"Do I look like I'm kidding? C'mon, let's go eat, there is this place right down the road that makes fried cauliflower."

"Let's ride the bikes, it's gorgeous out." We jumped on the bikes.

"Oh, wait, let me tell you about the bikes real quick. Alec doesn't do anything inside the box, anything. "Here, help me fold it out, Derek."

"Fold what?"

"The bike."

"Huh? How much did you pay for that crazy gadget," I asked as I curiously started trying to unfold this miniature contraption.

"It wasn't that much," he said.

"What a strange-looking machine. Only you, Alec."

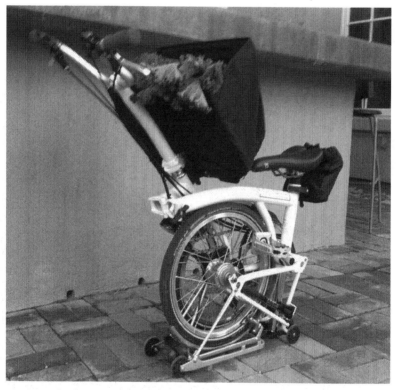

i never could figure out how to unfold Alec's bike

Walking into the restaurant was heavenly—it smelled just fantastic. There was no need for menus, Alec is a regular.

"We'll take two orders please. You can eat your own, can't you, Derek?"

"Absolutely."

"Here you go guys, enjoy!"

The fried cauliflower was probably one of the best things I've ever tasted. "Oh my god, Alec, the pine nuts on this are amazing."

"I told ya, Derek."

The next morning I had woken up stressed, as I knew I would have to make some adjustments in my life; not only my health, but also my children, my career, and emotional welfare all needed my full attention.

"See you later today, Derek, it's sunny out, enjoy the pool," Alec bade me, while doing his happy trot towards the door.

"See you later, Alec."

"We're having dinner tonight with friends, Derek, be ready by 7:00 pm.

"Okay, have a good day."

I stood in the middle of this magnificent foyer looking up the long, circling stairway. It's really quite a view, as the entire ceiling is painted with clouds, and the walls winding up the stairway are also painted in a unique way, like windows and nooks painted right into the wall. I had never seen something of the sort.

The house was quiet. I walked up the stairs to grab a towel. The sun was out and I was eager to play out in the pool. Walking outside into the courtyard has this overwhelming citrus smell. There are 75 lemon trees that surround the entire fenced in backyard, and 100 rose bushes scattered throughout. Basically, I felt like I had just entered fantasy island, a bit surreal to me, as I have never lived in such comfort.

I explored the pool, and even made a valid attempt to swim a few laps to ensure I was getting in some exercise, even though I was in healing mode. I ran back in the house to grab my shades, still not a sound anywhere to be heard. I was loving the peacefulness of Alec's home.

There's no one around, why not, asking myself the ultimate question when lying out in the sun: clothes on, or off? I think it's time I start living a bit more outside the box, and what a perfect opportunity—I mean, c'mon, who wouldn't? The house is surrounded by nine-foot walls, lemon trees everywhere, and roses coming out of my ears.

There is something about lying out in the sun naked when you know it's not your normal or daily habit; it's just kind of exciting to be honest.

I put my headphones on and began to eat the best peach of my life. Alec always keeps fresh fruit on the counter from the farmers market, another frequent stop for us on Saturday mornings.

It was perfect. The sun was beating down on my body, and the smell, seriously, the lemon trees and roses together created the ultimate outdoor aroma.

I texted Alec, "I'm never leaving your house."

"Enjoy yourself, Derek," was his response.

I felt eyes watching me, or maybe it was just nervousness about being naked somewhere other than the privacy of my own home; regardless, I was enjoying this "outside the box" moment.

I needed some more water; not bothering to take my headphones off, I made my way towards the kitchen entrance.

Those eyes that I had felt watching me a few moments back just became the truest moment of déjà vu if I've ever had one.

"Oh, god, I'm so sorry, I'm...."

"You're naked!" she insisted, with somewhat of an "It's okay" expression.

"Um, wait, let me grab a towel." I think she was trying very hard not to laugh at my nervous reaction.

I turned and it seemed like I had just started a walk of shame that seemingly took forever, although just thirty feet to my chair was my towel thrown over the back of my lawn chair. Each step felt as if I was never going to get there fast enough—I was seriously embarrassed.

Walking toward her now with my towel as my shield, I introduced myself, as did she.

It was the maid. I should have figured. A house this size has to have some caretakers involved.

She had been cleaning for about an hour before I approached her in my birthday suit, and I'm guessing those eyes I had felt watching me had quite the show to watch from the second floor overlooking the pool area.

I apologized probably five times. She smiled and told me to have a good day, as her work was done for the day. I wished her well, and off she went.

Okay, it's clear, not a mouse in the house. I went back to my lawn chair, took my towel off, and, once again, went naked in the sunshine.

Headphones back on, I grabbed another peach and closed my eyes.

Twenty minutes or so passed by, it was getting really hot now.

What the heck is that wind? Why is it blowing only on the back of my head?

There is no way this is happening, and sure enough.

The gardener had been blowing the leaves out of the backyard right behind me, and because I had the headphones blasting, I had no idea.

Once again, busted. I put my shorts on and decided to go for a bike ride—I just couldn't handle a third surprise.

My visit to Alec's was working, I was healing. There were reflections on what could have been: the baseball career, a martial arts fighter—hey, maybe Grandma was right, I probably should have learned to play the organ.

But that was in the past. Now, it was time to get back to being the father I had always tried to be for my three children.

THIRTEEN
Short Circuit

The defeated ultimate fighter, still sprawled on the canvas, was "coming to"; someone shouted as his head bobbled like a broken doll and drool teemed down his chin. Watching a man that size flail into a full blown seizure seemed to amplify the visual effects of looking in.

I felt noxious just watching his body struggle to gain control, it brought back memories of hitting my head as a child. Did I lie there and shake like that with people looking over me?

It bothered me that the fans in the crowd were screaming "Tear his head off!" and "Smash his face!" and then it happens. The fighter gets caught with a crushing blow that sends him into another world. The crowd quiets. I've grown up a competitive martial artist since early childhood. I was taught not only the discipline it takes to be the best athlete possible, but I was also taught to be compassionate and caring for the individual I was competing against. A handshake before a competition, then it's game on during the match, and when finished, another handshake or hug exchanged as proper camaraderie.

They were holding his head up, his body still lifeless on the canvas. "He's going to be okay," the relieved corner told everyone around him. It seemed they were saying the fighter was okay to ease the nervousness of everyone looking in, but the look in their faces seemed to say differently. Waving smelling salts beneath his nose for several seconds suddenly got a response; as he jerked his head away from the poignant smell, you could see sudden relief in the corner team. "He's okay" the trainer says loudly once again.

Maybe.

Earlier in the week, I had asked my brother Dino and Mike if they wanted to drive to Casper, Wyoming, for the ultimate fighting championship. I had previously attended the show's third installment in North Carolina for Helio Gracy's retirement announcement. Helio is the father of Brazilian jujitsu practitioner, Royce Gracie, someone I had admired very much as an athlete.

"What do you think, Mike, should we leave Tuesday for Wyoming?"

"Dude, that's a really long drive for a two-hour fighting event."

"C'mon, it will be fun; you, I, and Dino can take turns driving."

"Let's do it!" he relented, grabbing me in some sort of concocted choke hold to express his excitement. We would often have shop scraps as we called them. A boyish wrestling moment, usually at the end of the day, right in the middle of the shop. It would get a little gnarly at times, although the gentleman's agreement was in force.

The drive to Casper, Wyoming, was flat and boring. Driving through the Midwest is usually colored by rows of cornfields, tons of bugs hitting the windshield, and that dreadful humidity going through South Dakota and Nebraska.

In the early years of professional mixed martial arts fighting, it was intriguing that spectators sometimes thought the results were preordained and the action choreographed, along the lines of professional wrestling. Nothing could be further from the truth, but the history of contemporary ring battle to that date had been dominated by boxing where, occasionally, spectators are 'treated' to spectacular knockouts, but most bouts are attritional.

With barely padded fists, knees, and feet flying in mixed martial arts fighting competition, capitulation can come very swiftly. Hey, it's not the movies, we used to explain: you get hit hard and directly a couple of times in (bare) hand-to-hand combat and that's it for most people, even elite athletes.

Having been knocked out or into another dimension more than a few times over the years, I've often found myself empathizing with fighters, understanding that sickening moment when you compute something is wrong, sense the rush of sound, see bursts of color, and an awful whitewash, and try to adjust as everything seems to slow down amid a creepy silence.

When I watched that fighter lose consciousness, I felt like I was aware of every sensation he was experiencing, except perhaps the numbing fear he must have felt when he first glanced at his opponent; everyone seemed intimidated by this guy they called Tank .

Over the years, the more familiar I became with the experience of head trauma, the more I came to grasp how little we know about what actually happens when the lights go out or the room gets kinda fuzzy. Doctors, I've since learned, agree.

It's a mysterious world in there and most of the secret stuff happens without our permission or knowledge. Yet, for the longest time, even before I jumped into the shallow end at Bill's, I had the nagging feeling my noggin was undergoing occasional repair and renovation.

The headaches, angst, depression, tiredness, and my inability to make decisions that should have come quickly, easily, and without endless second guessing were all part of it. But those issues had been with me since I was about seven, so in my adult years, when I did finally obtain a modicum of concern for my own well-being, they weren't always standout problems that might prompt a doctor's visit.

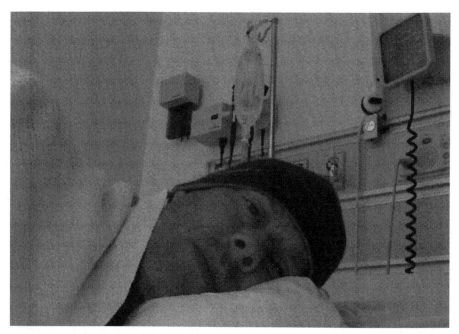

laying in the emergency room in new york

I only started to connect a few dots after the swimming pool incident in 2006, though initially, trying to make sense of what happened and why it happened weren't options. Playing music, especially during those first few weeks, was an intensely emotional experience. In fact, my major focus was to somehow open a tap and let these insistent feelings flow. I wasn't interpreting anything or even making choices, I didn't have that critical or creative expertise.

Each time you laugh or cry, you don't immediately take a step back in order to evaluate the psychological and biological factors in play. Obviously, the unannounced and completely weird onset of musical ability in middle age raises a few obvious, urgent questions, but, in the midst of it, you want to experience what's going on rather than instantly analyze it.

Where do you start, anyway? Mom's suggestion that it was a gift from God was as good an explanation as any. And, depending how you look at the world, it still might be, regardless of what happened in my brain.

For a while it was enough for me to surmise and generally accept that the collision between head and concrete that day was freakily 'to blame' and something from which I would recover. The sudden onset of my musical prowess was a temporary symptom like nausea. Indeed, for a long time (perhaps to this day) I worried it would disappear overnight.

But the sense that it had been a long time coming grew on me. Sure, the pool incident and the subsequent rebooting of my consciousness were decisive factors, but the run in with the monkey bars, the tumble off the truck after baseball, karate kicks to the head, popping pills, smoking weed, the death of best friends, the tumult around the disintegration of my marriage, and the loss of everything I owned have something to do with it. I somehow know this.

Part of me still doesn't want to know the precise how and why. Even before the constant burn of curiosity set in and a desire to find a way to explain myself to skeptical friends and acquaintances got to me, I suspected any investigation would likely lead down a poorly defined path in the direction of dark conclusions.

I was right.

FOURTEEN
Making Sense of It

Back in 2006, I was vaguely aware of people with extraordinary talents, like the guy who can draw a city in minute detail after flying over it, or others who, after an illness, develop abilities they didn't display previously, but the term "savant" wasn't in my vocabulary—really, I admit ignorance—to me it sounded like something you'd buy at a French bakery.

My cursory internet searches in the weeks after the pool incident, however, pointed to savants, or savant-like behaviors as being of relevance to my situation.

Savants, by one common definition, are people with disabilities who display extraordinary talent, usually in one discipline, in stark contrast to their overall handicap. Fifty percent of them are autistic. The rest, it's usually trauma induced, head injury, lightning strike, serious illness, etc....

There is something about the obsessiveness and repetition often associated with savant behavior I can relate to. Those grueling daily training drills for baseball as a child were some of the most strangely satisfying hours of my life, and now, I can fully appreciate the overwhelming desire to focus on one thing. After the accident, playing the piano was more than an itch I had to scratch: it was something over which I had limited control.

I didn't really feel I had a choice not to play, and when I tried to coordinate what came out, well, it was the musical equivalent of attempting to single-handedly herd thousands of cattle. I'd successfully play what was immediately in front of me (largely thanks to the flowing black and white squares), but I couldn't really get to the other stuff, even though I suspected it surrounded me.

167

I was unable to escape those black and white squared images pretty much around the clock, and, today, they seem to be going at a nonstop pace every minute of each hour.

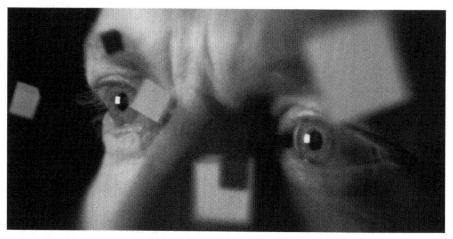

seeing black and white musical blocks 24 hour a day

That odd phenomenon, I gradually learned, could be interpreted as a form of synesthesia.

Broadly speaking, synesthesia is a condition that generates unusual sensory reactions. In some instances, the stimulation of one sense, say hearing, might initiate a reaction in another, for example, sight. Thus, on hearing a particular sound, the person has a specific visual reaction, like seeing the color red and tasting cherries.

I hadn't thought of it much before the ubiquitous images of the black and white squares became part of my life, but back as far as I can remember, I have on occasion made sense of the world around me in seemingly illogical ways, sometimes involuntarily engaging the 'wrong' senses.

I recall as a child when I sensed I could taste things I looked at, or sometimes I would associate colors with letters or words, particularly the taste of car exhaust when overly angered. Even now, it's not only the black and white key images that impose themselves. The hearing and light sensitivities I developed after the accident aren't only triggered by sound and light conditions. Other factors, smells, for example, might prompt a reaction with my hearing and, on occasion, certain sounds initiate a visual response (usually making lights harsh).

I don't have an absolute conviction that all of this has anything to do with what has happened more than six years ago. I'm quite willing to concede under interrogation some memories might be related to bad weed I smoked as a kid, but it's odd that it's been with me most of my life and still impacts me.

When I started poking around for documentation of experiences such as mine, I wasn't looking for labels or conditions to brand myself with—I'll leave that to the experts—I just wanted to know who else this had happened to.

What's more, regardless of my affinity with savantism, I had a tough time making a connection between what was going on with me and the traditional 'definition' of a savant.

I've never been diagnosed or suspected to be autistic or on the autism spectrum, and the ability I suddenly and inexplicably displayed isn't necessarily staggering in its complexity or execution.

Yes, I can now play complete and complex pieces of music on the piano, but it is the sudden emergence of this ability rather than the level of my ability that is extraordinary.

on set with Beverly for Canada AM appearance in Toronto

This is an important distinction, and one I find myself detailing over and over again, oftentimes at the risk of sounding like I'm scrambling to qualify myself.

"Savants display incredible ability," one musically astute observer noted. I, on the other hand, play with three fingers on each hand and my performances are technically flawed and less complex than most concert pianists.

And I offer nothing in my defense other than to say I wish I was better than I am and I promise to strive to improve. One of the most frustrating areas for me to deal with is not being able to capture every single note that flows by. At first, I was so eager to capture, or release, every note played with precision that it became physically tiring, not to mention that it was emotionally wearing me out. Even though I understand I am trying to accomplish the impossible by not missing any music notation, in my mind, I wake up each day eager to capture every bit I can.

Later in these pages, I'll detail what several leading experts have to say about savantism and their take on my situation through savant-focused lenses, but as the amateur sleuth, I see parallels between my experiences and those of a diverse mix of people—some classified savants—who seem compelled to focus on a previously underexplored or undiscovered skill in the wake of a brain injury or illness.

Brain aneurysms, tumors, frontal lobe deterioration, Alzheimer's and its apparent relative chronic traumatic encephalopathy (CTE), even Parkinson's disease, play roles in the transformation of these lives.

From corporate bankers who tossed in their Wall Street gigs to become visual artists after their brains were effectively changed by illness, to the radical remaking of a middle aged woman, convinced after a brain aneurysm that she had a complete, vivid, and real memory of herself as a male Vietnamese farmer.

There are also scores of cases documenting dementia patients suddenly developing conspicuous and sometimes uncommon skills, or taking on new 'identities' usually as their lives narrow to become slivers of former existences.

And there are apparent bits and pieces cases like me. We (thirty of us), the loose ends, had physical traumas before seemingly returning to normal—like the guy in upstate New York who was struck by lightning and immediately felt the need to learn how to compose and play music, and the furniture salesman in Washington State who turned into a geometry whiz after being the victim of a bashing.

A few years ago, despite my suspicions my brain had been rumbled a few times over the years, I started to think of myself as belonging to this separate and rare group: "neurotypicals" who escaped paying the price of a serious brain injury for the acquisition of a wondrous talent.

Sure I sustained some hearing loss, I was tired a lot, headaches (still) bedeviled me and I collapse occasionally—those damn fluorescent lights in supermarkets—but I wasn't dealing with damage so extensive that it required massive rewiring. After all, it was only a concussion.

Right?

FIFTHTEEN
In All Of Us?

I was familiar with many people growing up in competitive sports that suffered a head trauma. A kick to the head during a karate competition, colliding into another outfielder in full sprint for a pop fly, the smashing sound of two football helmets connecting with full force, and then of course, there is diving. Although playing witness to many of these injuries, it wasn't until my recent head trauma that I seriously began investigating this fairly quiet topic.

More than 1.3 million Americans report suffering a concussion annually, although it's anyone's guess how many hundreds of thousands don't come to the attention of medical facilities. Anecdotally, at least, there are very few people I know who have played sports and not been dazed at some stage.

Yet, if you're like I was, you're probably under the impression that most who take a head knock don't seem to be dramatically impeded outside the headache, nausea and an inability to participate in post game drinks. Stick a cool towel on their face, get them to lie down and take it easy for a while before getting back to it. That's not medical advice, just a shallow observation. Of course doctors, with all their education, knowledge and stuff disagree vigorously.

"First of all, we don't really know what a 'mild' concussion is. There is really no such thing as a mild head trauma," said Dr. Douglas Smith, director of the Center for Brain and Injury Repair at the University of Pennsylvania. "However, we have been looking at patients who traditionally have been considered mild concussion cases and found at least 15 percent have cognitive dysfunction for at least months if not years, after injury."

Dr. Smith and his colleagues at Penn State are leading the way in looking at traumatic brain injuries—including concussions—which is the main cause of death and disability for those aged under-45 in the United States with 100,000 killed and 500,000 permanently disabled annually. More than 5.3 million Americans live with a disability stemming from head trauma at a yearly cost of $30 billion to the nation.

While there long has been study into major head trauma and injuries such as hematomas (blood clots), fractures and contusions (brain bruising) concussions have largely flown under the radar (or is it the MRI?) until fairly recently.

In part it's because the impact of concussion is difficult to study. In particular, diffuse axonal injury, sometimes caused by mild head trauma, is especially hard to detect and monitor, but can be devastating. Axons, sometimes referred to as nerve fibers, conduct electrical impulses in the brain.

"It's kind of invisible for noninvasive imaging," Dr. Smith said. "The human brain is unique in having large white matter domains where the axons are, making them hard to detect."

For many decades, my simple suggestion that most head trauma be treated with a cool towel, maybe a pain reliever and a good lie down, was pretty much the standard of care. Serious head injuries seemed rare, obvious, and largely restricted to car crashes, boxing bouts, and vicious assaults.

Not true.

The idea, for example, that the only sports where competitors are at acute risk are the fighting arts, especially boxing, has been blown out of the ring by recent revelations from ex-National Football League players who have logged more than 3000 suits against the sports' governing body over head trauma related ailments, especially chronic traumatic encephalopathy (CTE). Soccer, hockey even baseball are embroiled in similar cases.

A number of ex-player suicides helped further focus attention on head trauma-related injury and illness. And it's not just athletes involved in high impact, elite sport: junior competitors such as teenage girls playing soccer are a focus of particular concern for medical authorities, and with this sports initiated focus comes a greater awareness of pervasive and potentially dangerous concussions in the general community. The return of a generation of soldiers to home soil has also fueled fresh investigation into head trauma.

"This is a silent epidemic," Dr. Smith said.

CTE is a degenerative disease often diagnosed in those who have suffered multiple concussions. Its symptoms resemble those of Alzheimer's, although the onset is often in people of middle age (their forties) rather than the elderly.

"CTE is just an evolution from dementia pugilistica or punch-drunk syndrome that has been diagnosed since 1928," according to Dr. Smith. "People who study this have seen it coming in vast numbers for a long time, but it seems to have taken society by surprise."

It's not only CTE that is of concern. Concussions in themselves are potentially devastating, and that contention is growing in strength as better imaging and diagnostic tools become available.

"We are not yelling 'Fire!' in a crowded theater," said Dr Smith, a dedicated football fan, "but we know enough about so-called mild head trauma now to be able to say it needs to be diagnosed and treated carefully and completely."

I have sifted through much material in hopes of truly discovering my own unanswered questions, and after all said and done, I tend to lean towards Dr. Treffert's theory, "giftedness lies in a dormant state in each of us."

It's the "how do we tap into this special area" that makes me certainly most curious, and could very well be the question that simply will never be answered during my lifetime. It's almost an obligation on my behalf to continue lending my brain for study in hopes of playing a small role in assisting the medical community in discovering many unanswered questions that we (TBI survivors) seek.

Was it concussion number one that opened up that tiny window of opportunity for my brain to tune in differently? Possibly my second, or third head injury was the key component, I don't know, but the entire process of discovering new answers and information in regard to my own case is magically stimulating to me, and insists I continue my efforts as a test rat getting poked and prodded for the advancement of science.

I've always referred to my last brain injury as "lucky number seven." To me, all those prior head injuries were simply different keys trying to unlock the genius within, and not that I thought I was a genius by no means, but I knew as a child after my first head injury that something in me had been rewired, or as I often say "my eyes look through a different window." Not that I'm any different from anyone reading this, it was just apparent that something remarkable transpired in my brain after my first head injury.

Sometimes I ponder on the "what ifs." I couldn't imagine the stress and challenges I would have gone through as a typical kid if this gift was discovered at the age of seven. If at forty-six years of age and seven years under my belt with this discovery seems challenging, how would a child that age deal, or even recognize such a profound life-changing discovery?

Either way, I could go on and on as to the many "what ifs" and questions that go through my mind daily, and there comes a time when you simply have to submit to "not knowing," or, "I may never completely understand this gift."

My mind races every minute of my life, not only with many of these questions I have, but the nonstop musical composition going on has at times brought me to my knees from the physical and emotional wear. Imagine driving your car and not having to put gas in it, and you could just drive, and drive, and drive, and then you go to park it in the garage, and the ignition will not allow you to turn it off. I can't even begin to process how many millions of these black and white squares have passed my mind's eye in the last seven years. The doctors have told me at this point there is no medical device on the planet to measure such activity, although, I am confident that new tools are coming, and technology will allow us to discover much more than just sudden musical ability, or "accidental genius" as Dr. Treffert puts it.

"This is just the beginning for you, Derek, and even after six years of exploration in regard to your current condition, there may be several other 'gifts' that simply havent exposed themselves yet," as Dr. Reeves discussed with me.

"What do you mean, Doc?"

"Your brain has been basically rewired, Derek. There are way too many supporting factors in your particular case that suggest that unlocking the music is simply scratching the surface, and you may discover other peculiar changes that expose themselves as you progress through this journey.

"You mention a special connection when in the presence of other 'gifted' individuals. What do you mean by this, Derek?"

"I'm not really sure how to explain it, Doctor, without sounding completely ridiculous, or weird, or even godly if you will. I've heard some pretty strange things, Derek, why don't you try and explain a bit more?"

"It's magical, Doctor. It's happened more than several times, not just with Tony DeBlois, but with Rex Lewis (the seventeen-year-old autistic, blind, prodigy), but a handful of individuals, even the homeless, Doc, and sick children dying from cancer, and the little boy lying in a coma from a life-threatening brain injury, and....

i just couldnt get enough of this amazing young man, with rex lewis during filming at the mayo clinic

"Do you get it, Doc? I mean, how do I explain empathic and intuitive energy? It's so apparent that even when I'm in the presence of some, I literally break down emotionally, almost as if I have climbed into their souls for just a moment—it really is bizarre. It seems when touch is involved, like a hug, or handshake, that there is this magical transition of understanding between two people. I feel their sadness, I feel their hurt, and sometimes even feel as if I was crying for them, rather with them. Geez, I'm starting to sound pretty damn nutty, Doctor."

Dr. Reeves consoled me as I was getting extremely emotional in my attempts to explain this area of concern and fascination. "You, my friend, are a very rare bird," he would say, expressing true concern and interest in my thoughts. Dr. Reeves has that special bedside manner as a physician, and I felt connected to him on a personal level, something I had not experienced with other physicians when attempting to put my true emotions on the table for examination, or advice.

"There is a magical process going on in your very special brain, Derek," something so special that even the best doctors on the planet may not even have answers for right now.

"I don't blame you for not wanting to take medication to assist in slowing down this miraculous process, Derek. I totally understand not wanting to take the risk of possibly slowing down the musical pace of composition, or even the possibility of medications interfering with such a divine gift, but you are going to have to start exploring the options of finding a hobby, or activity to include in your daily habits that may allow your brain to put the brakes on this overstimulated brain of yours."

"I think fly fishing helps a bit, Doc. I seem to slow down, or at least my brain doesn't seem to recognize as many black and white squares when I'm trying to catch Moby Dick. Why are you laughing, Doc?"

"You have a funny way of putting things, Derek."

Let me step back to a particular moment when I was filming with The Discovery Science Channel for the series *Ingenious Minds*.

with the discovery science channel filming crew at the mayo clinic

As I was preparing to walk into Dr. Reeves's office for evaluation, I was having a very candid discussion with Toy Newkirk, one of the amazing producers involved in building the show.

"Derek, have you thought about how you will tell your children if in fact the doctors find something in your brain that could possibly be life-threatening down the road?"

"I have actually given it great thought, Toy. I suppose that is my reason for not wanting to know. I am very curious as to what may be in there when they look in today, but I've stalled this process as I really don't know how I would tell my children if I were to be seriously ill, or possibly even dying from a newfound tumor. I'm not sure if I really even want to know, I feel like regardless of what is discovered going on in there, that it's simply part of the journey, and I may be better off not knowing."

"But what if they find something horrible?"

"I think my children and family deserve to know, and I'm sure I would need their unconditional support if I were in fact struggling with a life-threatening medical condition." I began to quietly cry, tears running down my cheek as the cameras were recording my every move. Can you please not record this, pointing towards the camera man to ensure he knew I was struggling at the moment.

Toy handed me a tissue. "It's okay, Derek, things are going to be fine." They continued filming, as Toy had convinced me that it was all right to express my deepest emotions. "It will give viewers a true understanding of who and what you are, Derek, a real look into you."

breaking down on filming set just before getting my brain scan results at the mayo clinic

"Come on in, Derek," Dr. Reeves said, waving me into his office.

I was so nervous that I had to ask for a moment to myself. I was getting overstimulated from everything; filming was new to me, all the questions, not to mention the many hours of being on set with people everywhere. I was assigned a nurse to assist me in a short walk throughout the hospital hallways, in the attempt to collect myself before sitting down with Dr. Reeves for my brain scan results. If there has ever been a moment where I was truly scared, it was now.

"I'm not sure I can have you filming me while I get the results, Toy, it's just too much for me to deal with. Can I just sit in the room with the doctor for my results and you can interview him afterwards to get the clips you need?"

"We really need this part of the story captured, Derek." Toy was not only charming, articulate, and very smart, but she and I connected immediately when introduced prior to filming. She had me in her pocket, simply because I trusted her from the onset of this project.

with the lovely Toy Newkirk on set during filming for Ingenious Minds

"Fine, let's do this," I said in my most confident voice.

"You're doing great, Derek. If there is a moment during filming that you can't get through emotionally, I will be right next to you, I promise."

There is something indescribable about preparing yourself to be told that you could very well be dying from the tumor just discovered in your brain, and it's not even what was hard for me. It was the fact that I was allowing the world to look in with me during a very personal situation. What kind of expression would I portray on film if they did find something weird? Would I break down again and cry in front of a world audience? Would I collapse from overstimulation and emotional exhaustion? I can't imagine what it would look like on film if I did in fact collapse and to wake up with doctors, filming crew, nurses, and of course millions of eyes watching this entire process through their televisions.

"To me it looks like a fairly typical scan of a brain that's been beat up, but I don't see any signs of stroke, bleeding, and the presence of a tumor," said Dr. Reeves. I was overly excited with joy, and when I watched the clips of that particular moment, I could see the stress lifted immediately from my own being, it was somewhat strange to watch.

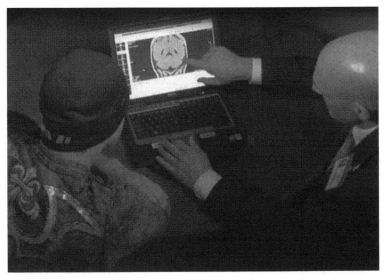

getting the brain scan results with Dr. Andrew Reeves - filming Ingenious Minds

Right before we sat down to film the results, everyone was busy hustling about the room, hiding camera cables, adjusting the background items, setting up the lights, and there was a brief moment when no one was listening to my casual conversation with Dr. Reeves.

I looked at him as if I was screaming, "Please, Doc, don't tell me I'm sick in front of the world watching, my kids will see this on TV."

Dr. Reeves could not discuss the results with me prior to the cameras and crew being set up to capture this specific moment. He didn't need to say anything actually, his eyes spoke loudly to me. "You're going to be just fine, Derek." I needed to feel that between us before continuing to film and he knew it.

"Concussion is not some sort of rite of passage, though most people will recover just fine … but it can change everything."

In just a flash….

SIXTEEN
Crash & Reboot

So maybe this concussion thing warrants genuine concern in terms of my long-term health. But could it also be part of a process by which I can point to an observable part of my anatomy that helped facilitate my sudden musical output?

What we need is a clear idea of what usually goes on in our jelly-like brains when they get a knock—all that 'secret stuff'. Which sends us back to our poor, clobbered ultimate fighter: dragged about the ring as he's lifted up under the arms by two trainers and poured through the ropes into the care of someone armed, no doubt, with a cool towel and headache tablets.

A candidate for CTE? Sure, but not necessarily a prime contender. As several doctors have outlined to me, the fact he was "knocked cold" doesn't, in itself, make his head trauma multiple times worse than others. In fact, if it's only my first concussion, I might be in better shape than a twelve-year-old who's fallen off his BMX bike a couple of times.

The 'lights out' switch is an injury to the stem of the brain. I'd always assumed if you're knocked unconscious, it's got to be worse than merely being knocked senseless (not a technical term). Apparently not: although a KO clearly isn't good for your health.

"You could lose consciousness because it's predominately a brain stem injury, but be perfectly fine once you regain consciousness," Dr. Smith explained. "As opposed to another person who has failed to lose consciousness because of the angle at which their head has rotated, but has sustained a lot of injuries to the axons in the hemispheres of the brain: diffuse axonal injury (DAI)."

I'm going to try and get my head around this DAI business and express it in lay terms, so with apologies to brain surgeons, neuroscientists, and others less addled than I who explained the process to me in great detail, here's my understanding of roughly what can happen when a large ultimate fighter punches you extremely hard in the head, or if you kiss concrete involuntarily, head the soccer ball in an awkward way, dive into Bill's pool, or maybe walk into a very large door handle.

Think of axons, the nerve fibers, as cylindrical pieces of putty. You can keep stretching and stretching these, but if you do that very rapidly, again and again the cylinder, because of "nonlinear physics," I'm told, will break. This is what happens in extreme cases of head trauma. The microtubules inside the axon tube are destroyed.

For the most part, however, the axons are stretched but unbroken (it's called shearing) when part of the brain moves rapidly, oftentimes smashing into the skull and rebounding. Though if the stretch is excessive, there can be an imbalance in iron levels, prompting sodium—or salt as it's also known in better restaurants—to flood the area. Excessive salt pouring onto what is part of the brain's network of electrical currents is not a good thing.

The axon's electrical process is disrupted and parts of brain can shut down. The lights really do go out in that neighborhood.

This excess of sodium prompts the brain to respond by bringing in calcium—a good transmitter—causing further disruption to normal transmission, as a highly electrical, or hyperpolarized, state is created. Calcium channels remain open, stimulating protein consumption: "Too much of this and you actually start to digest the internal skeleton of the axons," according to Dr. Smith.

As indicated previously, this takes place amid the relative camouflage of white matter in the human brain, and sometimes goes undetected and untreated.

"If you have a little swelling of a structure here and there throughout the white matter (of the brain), it's hard to see ... each are about a micron in diameter—it takes about 50 microns to be the width of a human hair, so it's not something that's impressive in terms of imaging."

Most of us will recover from this trauma and some will go on to be some of the sharpest minds in the community: doctors, judges, college professors, scientists, drummers ... okay, not drummers.

But if that brain gets another concussion, the chances of greater damage from, and less resistance to, head trauma swells greatly.

"One of the biggest risk factors for having a traumatic brain injury is already having had one," Dr. Smith said. "When you have one injury, we have found mechanisms that predispose the brain to an exaggerated response. So while you might have the same level of force in the second injury, the effect could be multiple times."

This is of special concern when it comes to children who may appear to bounce back quickly after a trauma to their developing brains, but are at acute risk if recovery hasn't been full and complete.

"Something called *channelopathy* comes into play if your axons are not working up to par," Dr. Smith said. "You're not getting what is called the conduction blast—the speed of the signal from one part of the brain to the other is not at a very precise level. Your axons add more sodium channels because the ones that are there aren't functioning as they should be.

"That's what happens with kids. They get a normal blast, but when another injury impacts them, the pores open up to sodium."

That's why our barely conscious ultimate fighter might actually be in better shape over the long-term than the preteen BMX rider. Our theoretical bike boy, as mentioned, has already taken a tumble twice, and if those falls have resulted in concussions, he may well be at greater risk of ongoing issues than the human punching bag with cold towel over his face who just endured his one and only concussion.

I was a little reluctant to ask doctors specifically what a brain with a history of about seven concussions might be dealing with, but logic tells me the electrical circuits in my brain have gone dark more often than a poorly wired farmhouse in tornado alley.

The changes that have taken place in my brain almost warrant a doctor's visit to bare bad news. I mean, c'mon, I wake up with these little magical black and white squares telling my fingers to dance on anything near. I suppose this would be my reasoning for not wanting to go for a doctor's visit. After the first couple years of adjusting, I did fairly well with coping with the changes, although it was the constant stimulation that has been most challenging. My hearing is slowly deteriorating, and I'm guessing in the near future I will investigate in hearing aids, but for now, I'm getting by.

There have been several stages through this process of having a new ability. I assumed at first learning of the piano that it was some sort of fluke and would possibly fade away. Then a year passes by and it's still there, and composing at a faster pace than the prior year. Maybe this was my brain's way of compromising for all the prior concussions, some sort of release. I'm still not sure when it comes to those explanations, and I have heard many.

I still like the way Dr. Reeves explains things to me, simple words rather than the big medical terms that I totally don't get. "It's like this, Derek: When you hit your head this last time, it opened up new window. Basically, your brain had a rewiring, and you tapped into an unknown area of enormous musical information." I had written down his explanation in my journals, as it sounded easy enough to understand.

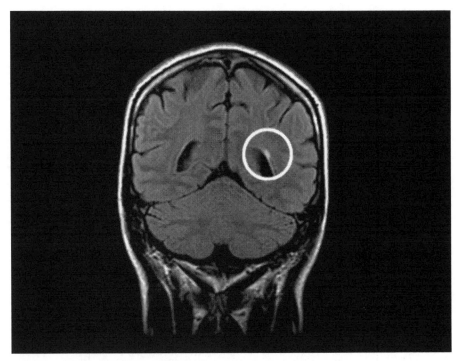

a total of five spots were found in my brain scans

It's one of those topics that most every doctor I have consulted with views in a somewhat different light, and I've come to simply respect each of them. Does it really matter? I suppose on the science side of looking in, yes, in fact it matters very much. On the flip side, it's really not going to make a difference in how I approach my each and every day.

I now live a different life because of this gift, and I'm not blaming or complaining. I love this journey, every second of it actually. I accommodate a different set of demands nowadays from my overthinking brain.

A typical day is usually filled with this:

Get up around 3:00 – 4:00 AM. Make coffee, even before going to the bathroom—yes, I like it that much, but only two cups or else I'm way too fast. I spend the first couple hours returning e-mails, and there are many, between business, family and friends, and fan mail; it's a handful, but I love it, as I find it really important to stay personally connected with those looking into my life.

I then try and take a quick walk, possibly 1-2 miles. After a shower, I'm usually in the music studio for a good three to seven hours, pending what other projects are at hand. I eat a quick lunch and move on to conference calls, scheduled interviews, and another e-mail review to catch up. Pending the time of the year, this is about the time in the day where I break out the fly rod and head to the water, and that could very possibly take me into evening hours.

Most of the time I will cook, especially if the kids are around. It's my favorite thing to do, and I can actually cook, but it's all in the presentation for me—yep, even if Mac and cheese. Then I'm back at my desk in the evening hours to work on promotional items, and yet another e-mail review, as I can't stand being behind.

I try and end most of my days in the studio. The piano has become my late night therapist. It soothes me to let the music go nuts before I try and close my eyes for the day. I don't actually even like to stop for a rest, but my body demands it nowadays, as I am forty-six now. I will go and go and go, then my body and mind simply get too exhausted and I shut down, but only for a few moments, as 4:00 AM comes quickly when you're not in bed by 8:00 – 9:00 PM.

**at Dog House Music Studios for the Skin and
Ink Magazine photo shoot with Sean Hartgrove**

I'm still adjusting to these changing items and it's taking time, but I am forever fascinated watching the process of which direction my brain decides to go each day; as a matter a fact, I can't wait to get up and start it all over again.

Some doctors battling to understand the mechanics of the brain with a view to shedding light on the secret stuff that goes on that can harm our kids and unexpectedly straightjacket our lives as adults are understandably reticent to speculate whether these still mysterious processes can also lead to weird outcomes like mine.

But the pieces that have come together for me courtesy of the recent intense focus on concussions add up to an important part of the blurry picture about what the brain has the capacity to do.

Dr. Smith speculated. "If you look at autistic savants, there seems to be a correlation between their skills and the lack of connection between different parts of the brain: it's the ability to communicate with itself."

"A fully functioning brain is busy with executive skills (organizing, decision making), and creative skills are sometimes suppressed—the brain is too busy. But if a pathway is blocked, perhaps these creative skills get a free pass.

by far, one of my most memorable moments. with prodigious savant, Tony DeBlois for the Haiti Charity

"I wonder if there is something potentially with brain injury that mimics autism, blocking some pathways to allow these other skills to emerge."

Maybe this is why my connection with autistic savant, Tony DeBlois, is so special?

But my biggest question is: Was this gift available to me after my first major head injury when I was seven, and I just didn't know it?

SEVENTEEN

The Puppet Act

Living with a gift invites many new opportunities and people into one's life. I've always been one to march to my own drum, so you can imagine that with many of these changes, I was reluctant to adhere to change, not to mention allowing anyone close enough to me to really *get it*.

Don't get me wrong here, as I have no problems doing what is needed when asked, I just have to believe in the message that is being displayed, especially if it involves sharing my story. Hollywood is a close circle of people, or should I say, all the important people stay close to all the important people—does that make sense?

You don't know how many times I have heard, "Oh, let me introduce you to my friend, he's a producer," or, "Once we polish your story up a bit and package you just right," or, "With the right management agency, you could be rich," and so on—I've heard many.

Polish what up? It is what it is, I told one agent as he tried to convince me to sell my life story rights for 15,000.00 dollars, "Do I look like my brain doesn't work, Sir?"

"Pardon me?" he answered.

"Listen, I was a businessman before I hit my head, and I'm still a businessman." I left the meeting after shaking his hand, thanks for lunch. I figured I'd at least let him pay for lunch since he had an extra 15,000.00 dollars.

There is a fine line when building a persona to display to a world audience, and I've chosen to display the real Derek. I don't find it necessary to fluff anything up, it just takes the fun out of the whole process of sharing something so delicate as one's life story.

I have noticed a different energy amongst many of the people who come to see me speak at an event, or perform a solo piano show. They actually come to look in, rather than being the typical crowd at some bar with a band on stage that no one's paying attention to. Oh, I know, my circumstance is a bit different and somewhat demands a curious audience, but that in itself is a tremendous amount of pressure.

opening for Stanley Jordan at Tippitinas Jazz Club in New Orleans

When I walk on stage, regardless if I am playing a musical instrument or not, there is a high expectation to witness something beyond spectacular—it's kind of built in, I suppose, due to the title *savant*.

What many don't really understand of my situation is this: My brain makes these black and white squares that move left to right in nonstop motion. These squares trigger my fingers to react. My muscle memory in my fingers is far from excellence, although getting better each day, just as any other practicing piano player would advance.

I use mostly six fingers when playing the piano: my thumb, first finger, and ring finger. Sometimes, my pinky will decide to smack a note every once in a while, but not too often—I'm working on that one. It pretty much goes for stringed instruments as well—it's the same fingers working, and in a very similar structure of fingering technique.

Something I didn't mention earlier was my memory—yeah, it's an issue sometimes. Where was I?

Oh, yeah, the pressures of a title. What I was trying to explain is that my brain composes music at a pace that the medical society is unfamiliar with—"off the charts," as Dr. Reeves said.

My muscle memory and playing abilities are far from keeping up with the musical notation being composed, although I do my best to capture as much as possible, whether it's recording clips throughout the day, or trying to figure out other methods of getting my fingers to perform up to par in hopes of displaying the music I see in its truest form.

I don't think I will ever achieve this task. Even though practice seemingly makes my playing slowly get a little better through time, I don't see my abilities of being world class in this lifetime. With that said, I hope this gives you a fairly clear perspective as to how all of this music stuff works with me.

visiting ground zero in new york city

I wanted to see were the twin towers once stood. This was a very important trip for me. I mean it's not every day I get invited to have a chat with one of my heroes, but I wanted to see a bit of the city before nesting in to go over all the details of my following days itinerary.

We sat on the park bench staring at where the twin towers used to be.

"I'm sorry, man."

"What, Jason?"

"I'm getting extremely emotional, man, let's walk a little."

Walking through a maze of turns to actually get to the site took about 45 minutes, which was okay—we were in no hurry to get anywhere. You okay, Bro?" I said, patting Jason on the shoulder?

"Yeah, I'm fine, this is just overwhelming to see." Jason is a soft man whose compassion for life is extraordinary.

After a bit, we strolled over to the underground transportation system. Let's head down to…," the cell phone ringing interrupted Jason. As he looked at the phone, he said, "Here, Derek, you better take this call, it's Barney Five."

"Hello?"

"Hi, Derek."

"Hi, Barney. I wanted to make sure you were in tonight at an appropriate time and ready for tomorrow." I loved this about Barney, she truly cared for my welfare—wait … I meant to say she really cared that Jason and I weren't on our way to some dark dirty bar chasing hookers and drinking all night. "Have no fear, Barney, that has never been my thing, and I rarely drink alcohol, so have faith." As we just left the museum of natural something, fair to say that our next stop was more likely to be a restaurant rather than a strip club. I'm just too old for that stuff these days.

We were in by a respectable 11:20 PM that night. "See ya in the morning, Bro. Are you ready for this?"

"I think so. I'm a little nervous."

"Get some sleep, Derek.

with jason drenner on the streets of new york city

I crawled into this amazing bed—seriously, never have I slept on such comfort. Maybe it was just because I had two beers and a full stomach—nope, it was the bed, I'm sure of it.

"Can I get a wakeup call for 4:30 please?"

"Yes, Mr. Amato, goodnight, Sir."

I felt very special this particular evening. Everyone throughout the day was so pleasant. I had my best friend with me, and I even got to take

Mom, and let me tell you, seeing New York was a wonderful treat for her, which gave me joy.

I leaned over to answer my morning wakeup call, pushing the phone entirely off the nightstand, as if it mattered, since there is never anyone on the line anyways, but I still always pick it up and say good morning.

I paced for the most part of the morning, as the music in my head was pounding extra loud that day. I was trying to figure out how to not have sweat marks visible through my shirt. It's not that I sweat a bunch when nervous, I sweat when I'm overly excited. I tried everything, from rewashing my armpits with soap, and even putting antiperspirant on, and I haven't worn that stuff in years, it hurts my skin.

I called down to the front desk. "Would you please send me up some scotch tape?"

"Yes, Mr. Amato, right away."

I was scrambling to the door putting my jeans on. "Good morning, Sir," he greeted me. "Here is your scotch, Sir. Um, it's 5:30 in the morning Sir."

"Do I look like I need a drink? Of course," I said, laughing over this one. "No, scotch tape." He did in fact show back up five minutes later with a roll of scotch tape.

If I can get this to stick to my skin, I think I got this sweating thing under control. Rolling about a half-inch thick nicely layered toilet paper stack was the answer. Taping the toilet paper to my armpit was a disaster, although it did get me by until I got to NBC.

My interview with Matt Lauer has been a personal highlight through this journey of mine that I will carry with me until they bury me. I find him to simply be one amazing man.

After the hoopla, several hellos to Tom Brokaw, Chris Rock, and a few other people who looked important; it was time to leave.

"Well done, Derek," Barney Five commented, giving me the big congratulations hug.

"Thank you, Barney, I hope it went well."

"You did marvelous, and now your life is about to change. I will have this book sold immediately."

Six months passed....

"Good morning, Barney, I wanted to check in and see how everything was going."

"I'm not having any luck, Derek, I'm sorry. What do you mean luck, we aren't in a casino.

"I'm getting nowhere with the publishers. Some want to rewrite with more medical information, some don't think you're a big enough star, some don't...."

"But you told me you had her and him, and him and her in your pocket?

"This isn't working for me, Barney, I've been working on this book for three years, and you promised me...."

"Derek, I promised you I would try. Let's do what they want and take another eighteen months to work it all out. I'm sure it will all be fine, plus you know you will get up front money from the big players, and I know that will help matters."

"Why would anyone have to be a huge star to write a book anyways? I will never be a huge star, Barney, there are fifty thousand of them. I'm a savant, remember, one of thirty, stars are everywhere, savants aren't.

Now, tell me why I have to be a huge star to do this project and share my life work?"

"If you want to make money, you have to do it their way, Derek. Let them change it up a bit, they will build the story into a beautiful....

I interrupted. "No wonder you told me not to quit my day job, you weren't planning on really working. I'm terminating our contractual agreement today."

I hung up after doing all I could to stay focused on being a gentleman. Barney is a lovely woman, truly charming, and very good at what she does, it just didn't work out as planned.

In the end, I'm proud of my decision. I wasn't about to let another entity come into a project that I have passionately put thousands of hours into building and paint a completely different story of my life. It's just not my thing, regardless of money.

I'm learning to curb my stubborn business habits, as I know it truly takes many people involved to make large scale projects come to life, but at this point in my life, I'm enjoying this journey, and regardless of the mistakes I may have made throughout the way, it's all in my own words!

I'm just a typical guy with an unusual gift, far from a puppet!

No strings attached!

Yeah, I've heard that one before!

EIGHTEEN
Almost a Son of Anarchy

I have been going back and forth from Colorado to Hollywood for the last several months. Well, let me step back a bit so you understand how I ended up spending so much time in sunny California. While visiting my mother in South Dakota. I was snacking on her famous bread pudding, which I beg for her to make every visit.

Of course, she had Dr. Phil on the television. I haven't really watched much TV the last seven years, as living in the mountains gives you every reason not to watch TV, plus I get way too stimulated watching so much war, sickness, death, murders, and just bad stuff.

We really do need a station that simply shares positive stories and information, such as SMILE TV, which is doing just that!

with sandy and the SMILE TV film crew

Anyways, back to eating my bread pudding on the couch. "Who is that guy, Mom?"

"He's a bad boy," whatever that means.

"A bad boy, why didn't they invite me on the show, I want to meet Phil badly?"

"I'm surprised he hasn't called to have you on the show, Derek, maybe you should have Jason contact his office, he would love interviewing you. He sure is good looking."

"Who, Phil?"

"No, the bad boy guy."

"You're checking out forty-year-old guys, Mom?"

"Well, yeah, he's a beautiful man. Still eating my bread pudding, and then Dr. Phil introduces the panel of "bad girls."

"She's the smart one, Mom."

"Which one? There are three girls on stage, Son."

"Her," I replied, walking over to point to the television screen putting my finger on her head, "her, the smart girl.

"Oh, you can tell she is feisty, Mom, in a good way. She doesn't seem to go along with the other girls and just stands her ground, I like that."

"She certainly is a pretty girl, Derek."

"I'd like to have lunch with her."

"Seriously?"

"Well, yeah, look at her, she's stunning, smart, and she has...."

"I know what you're going to say, Derek, it's her boobs that got your attention."

"No, no, no! It's not even that, it's her energy, Mom. She radiates kindness, and at the same time carries herself differently than the other girls on the show. I promise you, I am going to find a way to meet her."

The ease of Facebook has given many the opportunity to connect, find old friends, and keep people around you up to date on life stuff.

"Do you think she has a Facebook page, Mom?"

"How would I know, I still don't even know how to use that thing."

Sure enough, I found her personal page, and immediately shared with her that I had seen her on the *Dr. Phil* show, and I wanted to meet her.

She was fairly reluctant at first, and we spent a few months with typical back and forth conversations via e-mail.

There was nothing easy about persuading her to lunch, she just doesn't work that way. She is an old-fashioned girl, I guess, which was attractive to me.

She made it very clear that I can't always have my way, and to be honest, I loved her solid and consistent personality.

We decided to meet at an upcoming charity event to benefit Michelle's Place for breast cancer, located in Temecula, California. The event organizer was Gillian Larson, one of the participants from the reality show *Survivor*, whom I have grown immensely fond of. Actually, I have fallen in love with Gillian and her husband Ron, as there are very few people I have met with such compassion for others. They really are two special people to me.

with Ron and Gillian Larson in Temecula, Ca.

I jumped on a plane after all the arrangements had been made for my participation, and couldn't wait to meet everyone, as people from *Big Brother*, *Survivor*, *The Amazing Race*, and a slew of other reality shows had representatives present.

I spent the entire weekend with Tyana, the girl from *Dr. Phil* show, or, as I often refer to her, as "the apprentice girl." She was on that Donald Trump reality show also.

We ended up dating for six months, hence, my travels back and forth to Hollywood.

Not having a full time regular job when attempting to work in music and television can put a stress on any relationship, and I'm certainly much easier to deal with when I have a solid or consistent income, and through the last seven years while pursuing my dreams, income has been sporadic to say the least.

"I want you to go over to register, Derek."

"What do you mean register?"

"There is an agency that will give you background work on set."

"Like on TV shows?"

"Yes, real TV shows, silly."

"How much does it pay?"

I think minimum wage, honey, but they will tell you when you get all your paperwork filled out."

There was no way in hell I was going to work for eight bucks an hour.

"Get going, it's only 40 minutes up the road. I've gotten your directions ready for you, take the smart car today."

Sure enough, out the door I went in search for this agency that was going to make me a superstar and pay me eight bucks an hour. I wasn't excited the least bit.

Pulling up to the agency, I was pretty sure I was in the wrong area, as there were probably 200 people in line to the building I was supposed to go in to.

Nope, I'm not doing this, no way possible. I parked the smart car in a parking spot no bigger than a space one could fit a bicycle, definitely the plus side of driving a car that size, you can park the damn thing anywhere.

I sat in the car for a very long twenty minutes, staring down the walkway at all the people. Some had crazy punked-out hair, all sorts of different attire. It looked like a circus crowd waiting in some soup line in downtown Los Angeles, I was actually nervous out of my mind. I was going to call Tyana back and tell her it wasn't going to work out, but that would have not gone so well.

Tyana is a cut and dry type personality, no frills, just the facts, no small talk, just educated information to exchange, and I like that.

I got out of the car looking like a giant stepping out of a mini transportation module. I could just feel people watching me; I'm sure they really weren't, I was just a wreck and looking for any excuse not to get in that dreaded line. I was wearing a pair of jeans and a black t-shirt, as I wasn't so sure I wanted to overdress for minimum wage.

The line was actually moving along quite nicely, when I was suddenly grabbed by the arm by this beautiful young lady in a pair of jeans and big tall black boots, saying, "Come with me," pulling on my arm.

"Pardon me?"

"You're different, please come with me and we can get started on your paperwork." She took me aside and asked what kind of parts I was looking for in television work.

I had no idea what parts I thought I may be good at, this was all so new to me. "Um, I'm not sure to be honest."

"What kind of shows do you like?"

"Um, I don't really watch TV often."

"Well, they're going to love you."

"Who?"

"The casting directors."

"Why is that, there are hundreds of people here to choose from, why me?"

"We don't have time to get into all that, let's get you registered and a few photos for your folio." I went along with it simply because I had no idea what I was doing there.

The whole process took about three hours, after which I got in the minicar and headed back to Tyana's. I buzzed her on the phone. "I did it."

"You're done, Derek?"

"It was crazy, so many people, are they all looking for background work for eight bucks an hour?"

"Absolutely. This is Hollywood, silly, everyone wants to be a star."

"I don't think I fit in, Tyana."

"What do you mean, Derek? It's just for extra money."

"I know, but it seems so foreign to me, it's just a strange industry to me."

"Trust me, once you get on set, you will love it."

Tyana had a very special way of motivating me. I can totally see why most men would find her to be challenging; she is a bit intense, but I loved the challenge. I got to see a different side of this beautiful television personality, a side of complete care, and giving beyond any words I could mention in this book. Seriously, on a side note, this girl is the complete package, far more woman than I deserve. Being pretty in Hollywood is a bonus, but being smart, articulate, confident, and damn good at what she does is, in my humble opinion, "the girl to catch".

Not more than a couple weeks passed and sure enough, my phone rings.

"Is this Mr. Amato?"

"Yes, can I help you?"

"We would like to have you on set Thursday for a background position with a major television program."

"Um, what time do I have to be there?"

"I would suggest being early, so maybe around 5:30 AM.

"What do I bring?"

"Dress casual, and bring a book, sometimes you sit in holding for long periods of time."

"What the heck is holding?"

"Oh, IT'S an area you simply wait in until needed."

"Oh, I see."

After hanging up, I immediately called Tyana to give her the news. "They called today."

"Who?"

"The casting people."

"I told you, your look is a commodity, Derek."

"Oh, yeah, right, like my fashion trends just shake the world."

"Just do it, you will have so much fun, and you NEED the money, Derek."

"I know, I will do it, but 5:30 AM, c'mon, can't I go in later than the rest?"

"That's not how it works in Hollywood, Derek."

"I know, I just thought...."

"And don't be late, honey, they won't let you on set."

"Fine, I will get my stuff ready for tomorrow. See you tonight, Tyana."

"Oh, hey, what show is it for?"

"Something called *Sons of Anarchy*."

"No way, Derek."

Is it a good show?"

"I don't know, but it's a big show, and that's good.

I didn't sleep well, as my mind was not only making music at lightning speeds, but now I was trying to emotionally prepare for something I had no experience with. It had been a childhood dream to be on TV someday, and today was the day. Even though I had previously filmed with The Discovery Science Channel for *Ingenious Minds*, it wasn't the same, that show was about me, and it seemed much easier to play myself rather than that of a character being asked to portrait.

I woke up before the alarm clock like usual. This is habit for me these days. The day before any event puts me in a mode that is somewhat hard to explain. Regardless of the event taking place, I'm frantic in regard to being precise with time, packing accordingly, and the gist of it being self-preparation, getting my mind in check basically—and yes, it sometimes takes a whole day, and even several days, pending the event of course. I grabbed a coffee from the 7-11 just up the street.

"Hey, aren't you the guy on my magazine rack?"

"What?"

"Aren't you him?" she said, pointing at a freshly pressed *Skin and Ink Tattoo* magazine.

"Oh, that guy, yes, it's really me."

"Would you sign a copy for me, please?"

"Of course," I replied, trying to find a spot to put my coffee down.

"Thanks so much."

"Oh, you're welcome, thanks for the coffee!"

Doing 75 miles an hour in a smart car is like going 1000 miles an hour on a go-ped; seriously, every bump, and even a small burst of wind, and you're gone. It's really that small of a vehicle, and of course I would come to enjoy taking the little thing out for a buzz here and there, sipping my coffee and trying to grasp what is about to transpire. *Will I meet the stars of the show? Do I get to jump off a tall building? Is there...?* My mind was now in overload, trying to prepare. This is what I do, and some find it almost comical the process I put myself through for a simple day of work, and at times I'm even amused with it.

"Did you sign in, Sir?"

"Where do I do that?"

"Right over there, and then you will go straight to wardrobe."

"Okay, thanks." Walking over to a little shack seemed so Hollywood, as one would think I would have been sent into some beautiful private dressing area—nope, not so. I stood at the little trailer building with my slip in hand.

"Good morning," a gentleman greeted me.

"Good morning, am I in the right area?"

"You sure are, let me get your slip and I will get your clothes."

Another lady walked up to me and started dressing me right where I stood. Things move quickly when on set.

"Come with me," she said, pointing over to yet another building. "You're going to be a dog owner for the dog fight scene."

"Do I really have a dog with me for it?"

"Yes, this way, please. This is John. He will train you how to handle the pit bull that you will be working with."

People were everywhere—and I mean everywhere—it's amazing to watch how many people it takes to make a show. I pretty much hung out with Josh most the day. There is a lot of waiting and pacing, and more waiting, although simply fun to be around such excitement. It was now lunchtime, and I had done absolutely nothing but wait and I was getting frustrated, no buildings to jump off, no nothing, and certainly no cameras were pointing at me. Lunch was most certainly a highlight for me.

I kept staring at this guy with a scar on his cheek, put there of course for his scene, but I just couldn't place him. I sat down with Josh to eat lunch with somewhere around 200 people. It was some sort of controlled chaos.

"Can I sit here?"

"Oh, sure," I answered, as I moved over to make room next to me. It was the guy with the scar; well, most people call him Dave, I'm guessing. Finally, I noticed a familiar tattoo.

"You're Dave. I'm so sorry, it took me a minute to figure it out, the scar threw me off."

"Yes, I'm Dave, and you are?"

"I'm Derek." We shook hands and chatted throughout lunch break. I thought it was so cool that Dave sat with us background actors, rather the real superstars having lunch over in their private, air-conditioned trailer, exactly where I thought I was going to be seated for lunch.

"Let's go people, finish up!" a loud voice encouraged us to get moving along.

"Nice to meet you, Dave, I hope to see you again."

"Good luck to you, Derek."

It was a great start to my afternoon, as I have always liked Dave Navarro, he was a super cool guy.

"How late will we get out of here, Josh?"

"Oh, buddy, who knows, could be anytime, could be late. Yeah just never know." Josh was familiar to this kind of work, and to be honest, if I hadn't met Josh that morning on set, I would have left after lunch, as I don't have patience to just sit.

with Joshua Streeter, my partner in crime on set of Sons of Anarchy

Finally, it happened. I was taken out of the holding area, and was assigned my pit bull for the scene. It was rather quite simple: "Hold the dog leash and look serious," the guy told me.

"Like mean serious?"

"Just look serious, Derek."

"All right, I can do that." I put my most serious pit bull owner face on I could muster.

"Action!" the guy screams.

I stood there holding my dog, and then I turned and walked out the building with my dog next to me.

"Let's do it again!" the producer ordered everyone.

Once again, this time I put my real serious look on, squinting just enough to make me look mean. We are rolling. It all happened so fast, and before I knew it, I was ordered back to the holding area where I met up with Josh again.

"Dude, you got a pretty cool role," he said.

"Well, I sure didn't do much."

"Welcome to show business, Derek." We paced some more in hopes of finding a food cart. "Here, want a water, Derek?"

"Yes, thanks, Josh."

It's now getting into the late hours of the day, and still we sit in holding. "Does it always go like this, Josh?"

"Pretty much, you just never know when you're going to be used for a scene, so a lot of waiting."

"Wow, I had no idea! What a long day, Josh." The main actors had been brought in for a scene just outside the holding area.

"C'mon, Derek, let's go watch."

We walked out to the shooting area.

"Stay back, guys, if you're not in the scene."

Josh was working his way up front to get as close as he could.

"C'mon, Derek, just act like you belong here and no one will notice," and we did. It was amazing to watch the main characters of the show do their parts. They really do work their tails off.

"Mr. Amato, you're up, come with me." I followed my handler over to another building, which we stayed in for a couple hours. "Wow, I can't believe the sun is still out." The light was shining brightly through the building. I could have sworn it was sunshine.

"Oh, that's not the sun, those are lights, my friend," another background actor assured me.

We did another dogfight scene, although this one was set in a caged area and I was just a spectator. "Mr. Amato, hold this money and look like you're betting on the dogfight." I did just that, as I hollered, jumped up and down, and seriously tried my best to look like a gambler who needed his dog to win.

"That's a wrap, thank you everyone."

Everyone in the building began to applaud, so I clapped along, thinking to myself, *What are we applauding?* I guess it's common for everyone to do this when finished with the day. I was relieved, and I gave my new friend Josh a hug goodbye, and jumped in the minicar exhausted—and I mean exhausted.

I think the rush of being on set lasted about three days. I'm home. How did it go? Well, there is a lot of waiting just like you said there would be, but I met Dave Navarro.

"Did you get a part in a scene?"

"I did. I actually got two different scenes to be in."

"I knew you would have fun. It's where you belong, Derek."

A few days passed and I was finally coming down from the adrenaline rush. Like any excited person would do, I jumped on my Facebook page to announce my star status with *Sons of Anarchy*, and you could see me on the season finale in a couple of weeks. I think most of my friends were excited to hear this fun news, and some were simply a bit skeptical if in fact I had really been on the set of *Sons of Anarchy*.

"Did you get the mail, Tyana?"

"Yes, your check came in today."

I was so excited to just hold the check in my hands as proof that I really got paid as an actor—well, a background actor if you will.

"Is this correct, Tyana?"

"What, honey?"

"The amount?"

"Wow, you're lucky, Derek, you even got time and a half for working overtime."

"Lucky? Fifteen hours on set for this?"

"Be grateful, Derek, not everyone gets to be on Sons of Anarchy. Plus, you really need the money."

I deposited the 167.00 dollars as if it were some prize check; not sure why it felt different, I suppose simply being my first check from a bona fide television show.

I jumped on an airplane to head back to Colorado to see my children. I was missing them badly. I made sure to keep that paycheck stub close to me, and decided to use it as a bookmarker to keep my place in the book I was reading on the plane.

"Welcome to Denver," announced a voice with words I love hearing when going home. I grabbed my laptop, my water, and pulled my carryon bag down from above storage.

Getting back to the house was exciting, as I was so eager to share my superstar moment with my friends and family.

"Tonight's the night!" I screamed at everyone in the living room.

"What's tonight, Derek?" asked my brother, curious.

"My debut on *Sons of Anarchy*, dude."

"Oh, that's right."

"Someone make some popcorn, I'm sitting over here. C'mon, Sydney, sit by your daddy."

"It's starting, Mom, come in here and watch!"

"I'm coming, honey."

"Dad, when is your part on?"

"I'm not sure, honey, it's the dogfight scene."

"I can't believe you're on the season finale, Dad."

"I know."

"Me either, Sis."

I had never seen the show before, so I was unaware of the format, or even what to expect.

"Where are you, Derek?"

"I'm sure it's coming up, Mom, keep your eyes open."

It was getting towards the end of the show and I could tell everyone was wondering if this was just some made up story, as I am known for pranking friends and family often.

"Um, it's over, Dad, is there another episode after this one?"

"I'm not sure. I didn't see me anywhere, did you?"

"Nope."

I immediately got on my computer to e-mail my new friend Josh who had filmed with me.

"Dude, did you watch the finale?"

"Yeah, my parts were cut out, Derek."

"Bro, mine, too."

"At least we got overtime, Derek."

I was actually heartbroken. Not because my part was cut out, but I had to somehow figure out how to tell my friends and general public looking into my life that my parts weren't included in the final edit. I did my best to ensure everyone that I really did spend the entire day on set with *Sons of Anarchy*, and I'm sure most believed me.

I went to grab the book I was reading on the plane. I knew I could keep that paycheck stub as proof in the pudding, and I even wanted to frame it.

When I walked into the bedroom looking for the book, I had realized a moment that had transpired with a woman on the plane.

"I've always wanted to read that book," she said to me.

"I just finished it, it was fantastic. Here, give it a read." I handed her my book with a smile. She thanked me and went on her way, with my paycheck bookmarker.

It really was my introduction to working in television, and I fell in love with it, even if only for 167.00 dollars, and all because of the apprentice girl!

with Tyana Alvarado during my interview with Ability Magazine

Thank you, Tyana, for encouraging me to step outside the box and explore!

Oh, and one more note on this particular chapter. I didn't just contact the pretty girl on *Dr. Phil* that day. I also reached out to the badboy himself, Steve Santagati, and today he is my good friend!

It's not always just about the girl, just this chapter, as she really is that damn special!

NINETEEN
In The Doghouse

"Hey, Gary, how are you my friend?"

"I'm doing great, Derek. Wait until you see how the youth rock camp is coming along, you're going to love it. How are you?"

"This whole music business thing is so damn challenging when it's your only source of income."

"Oh, I know, Derek. I watch so many struggling and talented musicians come in here going through the same struggles. It's the biz, man."

"I know, but I think I am going to have to hang it up for a bit while I go find work. I have to create some income. I'm getting frustrated with the stress of it all."

"Why don't you come down to the studio next week, Derek, let's catch up and you can play until your fingers fall off?"

By this time, I had sold my car to assist with the daily incoming bills, so transportation has always been a little challenging to coordinate. The studio is an hour south of me, nestled just outside of Boulder, Colorado.

For the last few years, my travel has been fairly coordinated, meaning I basically either have one of my children drop me off at the airport or grab a shuttle. It's amazing when you don't have a vehicle how simple and quiet life becomes. You just don't really go anywhere beyond the typical stops to the grocery store, music studio, and airport; seriously, that's been my routine now for the last four years, and I've grown very much accustomed to this process, although a little inconvenient at times.

"I will try and make it down, Gary. I would love to see you, and I really need some playing time."

"Excellent, I will see you then, just ring me when you're on your way, Derek."

Gary usually ends his conversations with "Peace, man." I think the word "peace" was designed just for him—it just fits his demeanor, always warm and friendly.

I had met Gary shortly after returning to Colorado in 2007. I was looking for a rehearsal studio with as many instruments as I could possibly find. There was a handful of studios in the Denver area and all seemed to be fairly accommodating.

After meeting Gary, it wasn't even something I had to think about. His energy was infectious and we developed a friendship that I consider very dear to me. He gave me the instruments, my own studio room, and a 24-hour access key.

"Here, Derek, it's all yours," he told me, handing me the ultimate pass. That 24-hour access card overwhelmed me with complete excitement, as I knew I could play, and play, and play.

It became my "private space." Matter a fact, it became the one place on this planet that I could find complete peace. I would often walk in and just roam the hallways looking at memorabilia, as the clock on the wall affirmed it was 2:00 AM.

I would jump back in the studio and bounce off several different instruments, as sometimes taking a break from the piano would allow me some time to recollect myself. I get overly stimulated when I play, and, often, I need to just take a walk or go fish for a couple hours to break up the day—and evening.

Walking into the studio the next day around 4:00 PM, I found Gary in his always cheerful state. "How's it going, Derek?"

"It's good today, Gary. I worked all night and my back is starting to hurt from sitting so many hours on that piano bench.

"Go look in the other studios, there's different benches throughout the studio, Derek."

"This one will work," I said, tossing it behind the piano to replace the old one that was killing my back.

I continued working in the studio during the day, and just before Gary was getting ready to leave, he peeked in my studio room.

"How late ya staying tonight?"

"I'm not sure yet. I don't think I have a ride to get home."

"Do you want a lift?"

"Oh, no, Gary, go get some rest and I will see you maybe tomorrow if I am still here working."

I thought Gary had taken off, so I assumed my position behind the piano and continued hammering away.

Fifteen minutes passed by and another knock on my door. "Here, Derek, take this." Gary threw me a sleeping bag.

"What's this for?"

"You don't want to freeze, do you?"

"Thanks, buddy, see you tomorrow."

"Goodnight, Derek."

In this last seven years of my life, there have been many moments that have stuck with me. This was one of those moments.

I didn't have to tell Gary I had nowhere to go, he just knew. I had been squatting now at friends and families for the last sixteen months, and we had discussed this situation sometime back while chatting in the office.

Gary and I agreed on a full endorsement situation and I would have access and availability anytime I needed. This was a huge break for me, as there was no way I could have financially taken on the extra expense of studio time. It's very expensive when you spend up to 100 hours a week in a music studio, although Gary's rates at Doghouse are designed for the musician, which basically means affordable for all—well, most all.

I have done several interviews at Doghouse. The media loves having all the lights and big stage at their fingertips when interviewing me, not to mention it's where I am comfortable. Gary and I have been through this journey together, as he literally made much of this possible. We certainly have some fond memories together in this amazing place.

at Dog House music with Gary Lennox and The Today Show filming crew

We filmed parts of *The Today Show, Ingenious Minds, How Smart Can We Get, FOX TV*, Channel 11, Channel 9, and a few others, basically in my house, if you will. It's not often a man gets to say he enjoys being in the doghouse as often as I do, it really is a magical place to me, and I am quite sure Gary has smiled through the whole thing, right next to me.

I called my brother later that evening for a ride. "Hey, can you come get me, bro?"

"Dude, it's 11:30 at night, you're an hour away, are you nuts?

No reason to ask twice. "No worries, I was just hungry and everything close by is closed." I hung up; it was no big deal really, as I'm not often in a hurry to leave the studio.

I played for another hour or so.

As I walked over to the couch, I grabbed the sleeping bag Gary had so kindly tossed at me earlier. I was out of steam, my fingers tired, and my voice raspy from singing all day and night.

I leaned over and turned on the stage lights—red, blue, green—I love the colors and how it lights up the stage.

I sat and stared at the lights glimmering on the drum set on the stage, always trying to take a moment before closing my eyes to reflect upon my day.

The studio had become my home, literally, for those few days I needed a place to sleep, and Gary threw me in the doghouse.

His words rang in my head.

"The Doghouse is your house, Derek."

TWENTY
To Walk Away From A Miracle

Never for one moment have I taken this experience for granted, maybe that's why I strive so intensely to grasp every possible moment. When you literally map out almost forty-seven years of life with a pen and paper, the process insists you analyze every little fragment of each step you have chosen to take. It's almost intimidating, in a sense that your awareness is heightened in areas of your life that possibly weren't being paid attention to, or even realizing they were there. I mean, c'mon, it's all in front of you, eighteen of the twenty-four hours in a day, staring you down as if the book were screaming at you to make some changes, or, get it together, or, well, you know what I mean.

I can't even count the many times I have sat and pondered at the many different options I have with my life. What if the music went away, what would I do for a career? That's a fairly constant thought for me, as I really don't have job security.

I didn't just want to be a pro athlete when I was growing up. I had many interests outside of sports when it came to seriously plotting a game plan for a real job.

Public speaking has always fascinated me. I grew up loving the words of Zig Zigler and such, but I wasn't necessarily interested in being a motivational speaker, rather a presenter.

I tied in my interest with speaking with my martial arts background, and leaned more towards working in the safety training area with youth (rape prevention instruction, bullying, etc.).

Instructing many children throughout the country has been a personal achievement that I am quite fond of, although the normal career paths just didn't excite me enough, and I didn't have the patience for eight years of college to be a doctor.

The handful of corporate jobs that I have held have given me much—a steady paycheck, sharp minds to work with, and so on.

But knew at an early age that the path I would choose to take through my growing years would ultimately lead to something out of the norm. Well, it's not that I don't consider what I do today for a living normal, although it's certainly a bit outside the box, that's for sure.

I made some money and I lost some money when I was employed full time traveling throughout this beautiful country of ours, and not getting to really see much of it at all.

I had money in my pocket, a car, a home, and I was pretty much a regular guy with a job complaining about working too much.

Today, I travel for a different purpose. When I'm on my way to speak at a charity event, it's not just get on a plane, have a fancy *schmancy* limo driver awaiting me and get served fish eggs on crackers while trying to do a radio interview on the phone. I now take a meandering stroll to discover when I step outside to get on that plane.

"There's much to be done," is my usual saying before heading out the door! Now, on my way to the airport, I find it necessary to have friendly and meaningful conversation with my driver, rather than scrolling frantically through a cell phone texting and talking.

Then, suddenly, I see the old man sitting on the corner hunched over, his long, scraggly beard almost touching the ground.

"Please, pull over, if you don't mind," I always ask politely of course. I never order a driver to do anything, that's just simply wrong.

I get out of the car, asking the driver to give me a minute.

"What's your name, man?"

"Greg," he said with an almost dying moan in his voice.

"Are you okay?"

"I'm fine, man."

"Here, I have a twenty on me, please get what you can to make your day a little easier."

"No, man, I have money. That's okay, you keep that, young man."

"Here's the deal, Greg, I'm not leaving until you allow me to do just one thing for you. I just need to know what you need, brother?"

"I need someone to love."

"Like, for a long time, Greg, are you talking about like a girlfriend type of love?"

"Oh, no, I don't have time for that much love."

"Well, what were you thinking, Greg?"

"Can you sit with me like I'm a friend you love, for just two minutes?"

The driver who picked me up was not the regular guy I was used to seeing, although this new driver was totally cool. He was starting to nudge me a little to get moving along, and then his phone rang.

I listened in, as he was standing just three feet from me.

"Mr. Amato, I have to drop you off at your destination so I can grab another customer."

"How long will it take you to go do that?"

233

"Not long at all, maybe an hour. Or I can pass on the client call and stay here with you, but I believe the service will charge you another 125.00 if you still need my service."

"Heck, I don't even have 125 bucks, why don't you go do what you have to, and if you don't mind, just swing by and grab me, I will be right here in one hour."

I sat next to Greg on the curb.

"Guess what, Greg?"

"What's that," he replied, almost as if he didn't even realize the driver had left me there on the street corner with my suitcase next to me.

"I can love ya for an hour brother, what would you like to do? Do you want to go grab a bite to eat and chat for a bit?"

"I'm starving, but I don't have any money."

"Greg, you just told me you had money."

Greg went on to tell me how it hurt him when others would give to him.

"Well, I still have that twenty I was going to give you, let's go eat."

Greg and I walked down the street for a bit and found a small little diner. Greg shared his life stories with me, we laughed, we ate, and we loved.

When I sit down today and look into my life, I see a new career, a new day, a new everything actually.

There is no alarm clock, or a boss screaming at me to produce more revenue, or a client breathing down my back to figure out how to build his business for him.

It's just me and ten million Gregs. This is my job. There is no formal job description, there is no annual salary increase, no stringent attire demands of how I dress when at my desk, and the list goes on for a million miles.

I don't mind the struggles that come with building a dream into a career—and trust me, the struggles hit you in the back of the head every 40 seconds, which, in my case, could have me playing the violin, cello, banjo, and many more instruments very quickly.

A fall back plan has always been in place if in fact this journey were not to produce any kind of revenue.

Wait, I should rephrase that.

I have other talents that would allow me to find employment that I'm sure would be fantastic jobs, and, one day, I may just have one. But, for now, I am squeaking by, and I'm most certainly not losing any weight from not eating, as I have good friends and a family who believes in these silly dreams of mine to change the world.

at dinner with Lisa Jones, the national brain injury foundation charity event in new york.

You always hear people say, "I'm going to change the world," and then you ask them how, and many stumble with an answer.

If you're going to say it, *do* it. My dad always told me that, of course.

It's not a tough question to answer, actually. I think we can all change the world with a little more love. If there is an answer, I would imagine love would be right up there with the best of them.

I didn't get the opportunity to share love like I do now is what I am trying to say.

Oh, yeah, back to the limo.

So, after moving on from my most memorable moment with Greg, it was now time to put my game face on.

I get so damn nervous when getting ready for television interviews. I pace, I change my mind about what to wear ten times, and, of course, the always, "I hope they ask me nice questions"—rather a bunch of negative stuff, and, yes, I've had a few tough interviews, but most of them amazing experiences for me.

I really do like the lights, cameras, people everywhere; it's just a rush to watch everything going on.

It's that one moment when I can truly feel like, "This is MY circus show."

on set with David Pogue at Dog House Music Studios for the filming of "how smart can we get" with NOVA PBS

What's nice about this experience and newfound career with no job description is that the game face I put on every day I wake up to go to work in is simply me, the real Derek.

I don't have to change faces at all throughout my day.

Now, wait a minute, that doesn't mean I don't make different facial expressions when negotiating my performance rates, or something of the nature that calls for a change in face. It simply means I get to wake up each day in love the very man who steps out his door everyday to change the world.

If I had business cards, they would read:

> Derek Amato
> Title: - Love
> 800-555-5555

Yes, I'm that boy in fifth grade insisting the square peg would in fact fit into the circle hole, only if you sat and tried long enough.

And I sat for hours upon hours and still no fit. It wasn't going to fit, and I knew it.

There are so many different areas to my work nowadays, things I usually refer to as "stuff."

It really is the most multitasking situation I have ever attempted, and I know out there working in the entertainment industry are many people who truly understand the "one man show" "do all" description of what WE do.

During the last three years, I have become quite fond of working in television—whether it's an interview or as a background person on *Sons of Anarchy*, I have fallen in love with everything about it.

I have spent countless hours scripting and writing for what someday I hope turns into having my own show.

No, not like *Hillbilly Moonshine*, or *Wild Animal Hunter*—but a whole different level of reality television.

I hope to someday display a whole different view of how reality television should be designed and displayed, and I'm thinking you're going to love it. Plus, it's time we start incorporating things that structure interactive life learning methods, rather the typical drama everyone expects to see.

I dream to expose the gifted, the individuals who hide in the darkest of corners on this planet, those I know one can find. Someone so inspiring that you have to watch, and it's not even about that. What would happen if a reality show required audience participation, a networking panel of neighborhoods, allowing thousands of people to assist each other in this game of life? Gosh, that's a whole other book.

I would imagine by this time in the book you're starting to get it, as I am confirming with you this very moment, before you close this book for the final time, that the thoughts of me trying to fit that square peg in was exactly what you expected.

As Jason would say, "You're nuttier than squirrel shit, Derek," and I'm sure Jason is somewhere with a huge smile on his face just knowing that all of you would in fact agree!

I'm not exactly sure where I'm going tomorrow—that's the best part of this job. There really is something new around every corner, and I refuse to simply let go of living the dream of loving!

I don't think I will be walking away from this miracle anytime soon, unless the music unexpectedly decides to take a break.

I suppose that's when I will go get a real job!

TWENTY-ONE

When you complete the last sentence in a book that you have spent the last four years of your life writing, there is some kind of weird peace, and feeling of loss, all in one.

Almost as if I were ending this amazing love affair with the daily and vigorous habits that have become dear to me through this writing process.

So it's a goodbye, if you will, as I'm sure there will come a day when I may pick up another pen and paper.

To my children—Alex, Sydney, and Morgan—I am leaving this chapter blank, especially for the three of you.

It is my hope that you will spend your lives giving back and sharing love and life with many.

Throughout the rest of your lives, you will gather millions of words to describe your life journeys, and there will come a day when your journeys become my chapter twenty-one.

I am trusting that you will fill that final chapter with millions of wonderful words that reflect my joy for the life I have been blessed with!

Derek Amato has appeared on:

Ingenious Minds - The Discovery Science Channel
How Smart Can We Get - NOVA Science Now PBS
The Today Show
The Jeff Probst Show
Weekend Sunrise - Morning Show - Australia
Canada AM - Morning Show - Canada
Huffington Post Live
Fox and Friends
FOX Television
Popular Science
Skin and Ink Tattoo Magazine
Ability Magazine
The Guardian
Chat Magazine
The National Examiner
New York Times
NPR - Snap Judgment
BBC
NPR - Studio 360
The Edge - Australia
The John Moore Show
The Jay Thomas Show
Serius Radio

Supporting Organizations and Endorsements

Dog House Music Studios
Lafayette, Colorado.
www.doghousemusic.com

Community Water Solutions
Ghana
www.communitywatersolutions.org

National Brain Injury Foundation
Utica, NY

CORPBASICS
www.corpbasics.tv

Bad Boys Finish First Clothing
www.badboysfinishfirst.com

Elkhorn Fly Rod and Reel
Loveland, Colorado.
www.elkhornflyrodandreel.com

Get Fit 4 Life - Fitness & Lifestyle Wellness
Sioux Falls, South Dakota
www.getfit4life.org
605-212-3797

VETS ROCK
Atlanta, Georgia.
www.vetsrock.org

Jammin Jenn Music Therapy
Watchung, New Jersey
www.jamminjenn.com

Millennium Gallery of Living Art
Fort Collins, Colorado.

Katzenberger LLC. Home Improvements
Sioux Falls, South Dakota
605-941-7572

CD ROLLOUT
Los Angeles, California.
www.cdrollout.com

SIKGEAR INC.
www.sikgearinc.com

Sean Hartgrove Photography
Denver, Colorado.

Simon Hammond Photography
www.picsbysimon.com
Kitchener, Canada

Killer Image Photography
Dale Porter
San Diego, California
www.kilerimage.com

Everyday Beauty Artistic Photography
Lalena Kotasek
Colorado Springs, Colorado.

Rare Form Photo
ORANGE, CA
Hollywood, California.

Rose Pettibone Photography
Sioux Falls, South Dakota.

Josh Randall Photography
Ft. Collins, Colorado.

Gigi Marie Photography
Sioux Falls, South Dakota.

JUL 1 7 2018

Made in the USA
Lexington, KY
28 April 2018